FINDING YOUR WAY

CHANGE

THROUGH LIFE'S

HAPPENS

TRANSITIONS

CHANGE HAPPENS

FINDING YOUR WAY
THROUGH LIFE'S TRANSITIONS

C. W. Brister

PEAKE ROAD

Macon, Georgia

ISBN 1-57312-091-X

Change Happens
Finding Your Way Through Life's Transitions

C. W. Brister

Copyright © 1997

Peake Road
6316 Peake Road
Macon, Georgia 31210-3960
1-800-747-3016

Library of Congress Cataloging-in-Publication

Brister, C. W.
        Change happens: finding your way through life's transitions /
        C. W. Brister
        xii + 132 pp.   6" x 9" (15 x 23 cm.)
        Includes bibliographical references.
        ISBN 1-57312-091-X   (alk. paper)
        1. Life change events.   I. Title.
        BF637.L53B746   1997
        158—dc20   96-38532
                                                                   CIP

To Mark, Rhonda, Barrett, and Austin

Cherish the Past. . . .
Enjoy the Present. . . .
Remember the Future. . . .

CONTENTS

PREFACE

No one has forever. We each live in the crucible of change. In the past, I imagined that the gold ring of life's privileges rarely comes around. Now, I sense that there are many chances, choices, little deaths, and resurrections throughout the human lifespan. As we move fast forward into the future we plead with the poet, Ralph Hodgeson: "Time, you old gypsy man, will you not stay, put up your caravan just for one day?" The clock and calendar are relentless in marking epochs along the human journey.

This volume is your personal invitation to an examined life. Facing defining moments, when one's best judgment is tested, and finding life's purpose is a morally serious vocation. This call to reflection on your work of soul-care involves other persons as well. Your story is part of the universal story of humankind. And your influence can affect issues surrounding the common good.

As a member of the World War II generation, I recall the speed of Adolph Hitler's juggernaut war machine crushing central European nations. Centuries-old republics were swept away in the fury of conflict. A son of the South, accustomed to storied place, I went to officers' school in New York as a military service volunteer. Conflict's voice called millions of young men, not unlike myself, to leave hearth and home, education or occupation, and to chart new trails in the wake of war. Now, our location in history is only one cohort group of several contemporary adult generations.

Change happens and we try to make sense of life's new playing field. Through the years, I have sought wisdom for managing life's transitions. Personal experiences, life cycle theory, family systems research, biblical reports of passages mid generations, multicultural rites of passage, plus my vocation in the field of pastoral care and counseling, have inspired interest in transition management. We each long for certainty, community, and God's covenantal care mid life's passages. Our pursuit of a place in the created and social order is matched by longings of all "the others" for a home in our complex universe.

We live in the postmodern world where life is being redefined. When we say, "That can never happen!" contrarians argue, "Anything can happen." Life has a strange way of "jerking our chain" and forcing us to ask ultimate questions. Probe any issue to its depth, from speeding along the electronic superhighway to pregnancy after menopause, from USAmerica's craze with gambling to AIDS, and we find ourselves on a spiritual quest. We seek assurance that we have an anchor in this vast universe, a connectedness with God.

Time travelers are on a faith journey. We are each mapmakers, trying to chart our course toward some "promised land." Our stories are filled with excitement and occasional failure, anticipation and disappointment, hope and anxious longing. For many US Americans, life is a matter of luck—a spin of the wheel of fortune. They are guided by fate. Millions of others trust their creator for resilience and guidance mid the fragmentations of life. They sense their vocational journey is shaped by the hand of God.

Pathseekers live at the interface between present events and future outcomes—what I call spiritual homelessness and ultimate home. Putting our inner and outer journeys together, in a changing culture, is life's assignment for us. Noted pathfinders such as Mohandas Gandhi, Thomas Merton, Dietrich Bonhoeffer, Helen Keller, Golda Meir, and Mother Teresa discovered ways to nourish the soul while touching the world. Such persons encountered current events with a compelling vision of a new and different world. More than any other person in history, Jesus Christ, homeless himself, offered an enduring place to all homeless sojourners of earth.

I am writing to persons who seek landmarks to guide them on life's journey. In an era of warring ideologies and corrosive violence, stories of sensitive, visionary people can provide us wisdom to live by. I have gathered up the loose threads of various peoples' testimonies to managing transitions and woven them into a meaningful tapestry. With patience and imagination, you can blend your story into Everyperson's story to create a faith map for your own pilgrimage.

Change is a certainty on the human journey. Employees of a major television network awake to the news they work for a $19 billion merged enterprise. An electrician loses both hands in a high voltage industrial accident. An army engineer is sent from a U.S. base to keep peace in a foreign, hostile land. Children at play on a holiday are swept to their deaths by gunfire from a gang train of passing cars. Friends betray us. Another plane goes down. When crises happen, it is possible to become confused, cynical, and bitter. How easily we forget life's essential goodness and blame others for our hurts and disappointments.

We can have the perfect job and lose it, good health and develop a sudden illness, be enjoying a holiday and experience a near-fatal accident. An intimate marriage can experience neglect, abuse, infidelity, anger, mistrust, and then end in divorce.

When facing transitions, people can either adapt or resist. We fear loss of control. We examine options, sort out pieces of life's puzzle, search for security, and then try to "mark the trail" for future generations.

The pages that follow offer guidance in our universal search for significance and certitude. Because common ventures of life, such as marriage, often become risky propositions, we look first at the costliness of change—at its price tags. There are many notions of how change happens; so, a framework for thinking about it is proposed. As you look at your life, you'll aim toward a meaningful vocation, healthy relationships, and a hopeful future.

Let's admit it. Some changes can be scary. We need help going toe to toe with messy events. Some guides see only one way to get through passages—endings, questionings, and beginnings. Since individuals and experiences differ, this volume proposes optional routes for charting a course through major transitions. We shall create maps for individual situations and communal concerns as we go along. You may seek wise counsel while facing a difficult passage and profit by completing assignments proposed at the close of each chapter. Answering the questions will require intro-spection and dogged determination to change well. And group discussions may inspire new directions.

Some of life's most sustained searches come from our longing for clear identity-in-community, which I call one's "inner home."

Healthy selfhood remains an elusive goal for many people. They fail to experience the blessing and security of wise love and caring relationships. They only know a lifetime of conflict, pain, rejection, failed expectations, anger, loss, depression, and efforts to create a sustainable self.

Gaining the courage to become one's true self requires a heroic quest for the "land of inner home." Life calls us to authentic faith, true community, and wise commitment to our mission in the world. There will be fitful stops and starts. Despite detours, we search for the key to a true residence for the heart. Without spiritual energy, hopeful vision, and healthy effort, we may get stuck along the journey.

Stories to live by are a centerpiece of what follows. You will see yourself in these etchings—from childhood fantasy, to youths' predicaments, to adults' challenges. Life is here, though joined with death. Place is here, but linked with loss. Joy is here, yet splashed with pain. Above all, hope is here because of God's care and the ways of the Spirit. Find yourself in these stories. You may have to deconstruct some aspects of your own story and reconstruct other parts as you shape your future story.

No work like this is born fully grown. Capable partners have added texture and tone along the way. My warmest gratitude to Gloria—my wife, dearest friend, ministry partner, and wise companion on the journey of faith. Other readers who have responded to these ideas and enriched the work include Nancy Ellett Allison, Karl Fickling, Sarah Smith Boyles, Steve Lyon, Carol Childress, and Dale Brown. I have known and worked with many persons whose stories are related here. Some storytellers are named, with their permission. Others appear anonymously to protect confidentiality, though the incidents are factual. Abiding thanks to Lisa Bontrager, Emily Miller, and Sarah Boyles, loyal assistants and friends, who prepared unfolding versions of the manuscript.

Blessings on your journey,
C. W. Brister
Fort Worth, Texas

Chapter 1

CHANGES, CHALLENGES, AND CHOICES

L ife should come labeled: "Subject to change without notice," since we live constantly between the *now* and the *not yet.* Transitions occur all around us and inside us at personal, social, systemic, and global levels. Though a Rip Van Winkle mindset may deny life's upheavals, transformations occur in every nook and cranny of existence.

Some alterations delight us—a positive health check; getting the course and teacher we prefer in school; beginning a committed, creative marriage; the birth of a healthy child; an anniversary; a baby shower; graduation; a job promotion; or a winning season for some favorite athletic team. The opposite is just as true. We are dismayed when reversals come in our health, financial well-being, family relationships, institutional security, or government integrity. Extreme chaos creates anxiety as in events such as an injury accident, random violence, ethnic war, or a natural disaster.

Certain changes may be anticipated—for example, completing a course of study and receiving a diploma certifying one's competence in a field. Going to work for a multinational corporation requires out-of-town travel; so, get ready! A parent's declining physical condition may herald a future in a nursing center, with changing financial and care needs. Some events, for instance, a heart attack or stroke, are unexpected. Other alterations may be elective—such as accepting a job promotion, having plastic surgery for cosmetic purposes, beginning or stopping a romantic relationship, volunteering to work at an AIDS outreach center, or taking a vacation.

Change-free living is inconceivable. Some changes sneak up on us and catch us off guard—a drive-by shooting, an automobile accident, a diagnosis of heart disease or cancer, a coup attempt by rebel leaders, an apartment building blaze, an ethnic cleansing-inspired "Holocaust," or involuntary termination from one's job. Other events notify us in advance, as with the coming of a new Wal-Mart store to a region accustomed to hometown retailers; the merger of major businesses; or changed governance of a nation such as the Republic of South Africa after apartheid.

People in many lands are experiencing seismic quakes in governance, economics, lifestyles, altered boundaries, work and play habits, health care, family ties, sexual behavior, abuse of drugs, as well as in communication advances on the digital information highway. Some environmentalists question the sustainability of life as we know it on planet Earth. And we have become strangers in our own country following global population shifts to USAmerica.

Stories of lifechange on the street where we live—for example, a neighbor's death—may shock us into awareness of "the others." Too many sad stories desensitize us. We become hardened to the tragic dimension of televised reports where bad news is considered good news by media personalities. Reality disappears into virtual reality of interactive technology. Make-believe and myth become "manufactured truth." Digests replace history. The day's news must reflect spin and hype to impress us.

 CHANGES AND CHALLENGES LIE CLOSE AT HAND. We must consider them—the things that happen to others—because some-day they could be our stories, too. We are bound to "the others" in the web of life. It is time well spent to study their stories, from silent mutations to stormy violence.

QUIET MUTATIONS

Changes that come with the passing of time catch us off guard. Jim and Billie Webb have "suddenly" grown old. Now in their eighties, they have moved into an environmental haven called a retirement center. Billie was the first to falter, with symptoms akin to Alzheimer's. Family and friends thought she was on too much medication. Some days Billie seemed depressed and antisocial.

Jim carried on bravely despite Billie's reclusiveness until he collapsed one day and fell in their apartment. The doctors discovered near-stroke conditions, with blocked carotid arteries.

Surgery was ordered, and his blackout spells lessened. Jim still drove the family automobile for errands and social occasions. His family knew he jeopardized other persons and himself. But Jim would not give up his car keys until ordered to do so by the court.

Surrounded by creative retirees, these octogenarians want a new lease on life. They don't want to fall apart but to stay fit. They are brave persons with seniority and great faith in God. They are trying to hold their ground and stabilize each other in a confining, but safe, social environment.

Silent changes touch the lives of the Baby Boom generation. There are some seventy-five million of them in USAmerica. Rick Hernandez, in the age-forty transition and divorced, said, "I'm a nomad. It seems as though I live in constant change and transition." His ex-spouse and daughter live in another state, while his adolescent son elected to live with him.

"I would like to buy a house, put down roots, plant some trees, and stay somewhere thirty years," Rick noted. "But, I don't think it'll be here. That's just an ideal dream, but it *may* not be possible." His dream is the condition of millions of USAmericans as well as emigrants from many lands.

Susan described childhood separations and leavings that snowballed: "We moved twenty times by the time I was twenty years old. The longest we ever lived anywhere was three years. We didn't have real neighbors. I never got to make friends at school." While Susan's mobility seems excessive, it highlights our uprooted society.

Changes seem to multiply during the seasons of life. At fifty-four, Jan became a grandmother and experienced new sensations in her self-perception as well as in family ties. The biological clock had moved her steadily into the middle years. No more birth-children were possible for her; yet, a new generation was begun in her family line.

The ancient Hindu image of life features a key change at the birth of one's grandchildren. As William Bridges said,

> Until that time one has been in the *householder* stage of life,
> a time in which self-fulfillment and personal development
> have involved participation in social roles, family life, and
> the world of work.[1]

With emergence of grandparenthood, a person moves toward the reflectiveness of the *forest dweller*. It is a new era of introspection, gathering strength, and seeking vision for the journey ahead.

In Jan's case, there was a complex twist. The identical month of her passage into grandparenting, a new job opportunity opened. An administrative secretary, she went through the mixed emotions of welcoming a grandchild at the same time she was leaving all her fellow office workers. The farewell party in her honor brought her work "family" together for refreshments, speeches, hugs, and tearful goodbyes. Jan felt a lot churning inside. With only a weekend between jobs, there was no occasion for solitude and reflection on the road ahead. City dwellers have little time for *forest-work*—charting life's future course.

But changes involve more than quiet mutations. They may also involve admirable accomplishments.

HEROIC ACCOMPLISHMENTS

Early successes in life can change everything for a child and his or her family. Such is the case of eleven-year-old fifth grader Geoffrey Griffin, prize-winning author of a semi-autobiographical story, *The Magic Bat*. Geoffrey's 1,500 word mini-book about a young ballplayer's fantasy of slugging home runs with a "magic bat" was one of five grand-prize winners in a nationwide publishing contest.[2] The book relates the story of a youngster named Geoff who believes that a magic bat is the key to being a good baseball player. Once he found the perfect bat, Geoff no longer struck out.

For the season's last game, Geoff accidentally forgets his magic bat at home. But even without it, he hits a home run and his team wins the game. The young slugger receives a trophy as most valuable player, and his team wins the league title. After the game, Geoff discovers his magic bat lying on his bed at home. He observes, "I knew my coach had been right. It wasn't the bat that made me a great hitter. It was me!"

In recognition of his writing efforts, young Geoffrey received a $500 check and a publishing contract that includes potential royalties (if sales justify). He was eight when he wrote the story; three years later, he revised it. Writing is Geoffrey's favorite subject in school. "I write stories all the time," he said, "especially imaginative ones. I want to be a writer for sure." Geoffrey is like many other ordinary people who have done extraordinary things.

A fulfilling marriage may involve sacrifices and accomplishments, particularly when it calls for heroic caregiving. Jerry and Jane Songer's near-decade experience with her lymphoma reveals their heroism and devotion, as well as the loyalty of their faith community.[3] On the eve of the Songers' first anniversary as pastoral family of a congregation in Roswell, Georgia, Jane was diagnosed with lymphoma. They knew that some churches, when faced with the drain of time, money, and energy attendant to chronic illness, have found a reason to terminate the pastor.

But their congregants did not call for Jerry's resignation. "It has not been easy," admitted a senior deacon, "but I believe we have come through this experience as better people."

In time, Jane spent 130 days in the hospital fighting for her life. When a bone marrow transplant at Vanderbilt Hospital in Nashville was unsuccessful, doctors told her to "go home and get your house in order." They could do nothing more for her. Undeterred, the Songers prayed for a miracle and sought help from the National Cancer Institute in Maryland.

Jerry discovered trying to serve a large church as pastor and as caregiver to Jane was not easy. "Whichever place I was at a given moment," said Jerry, "I thought I should be at the other." Rather than facing dismissal, the Songers were supported by the love, prayers, patience, and fidelity of their parishioners. In the six weeks Jane was at the National Cancer Institute in Maryland, church members provided Jerry plane tickets to use for his weekly trips to be at her side.

Songer would not think of himself as a hero. Rather, he did what he thought needed to be done, though his wife eventually succumbed to the destructive disease.

 SOMETIMES, WE DENY THE WORK THAT CHANGE REQUIRES. Life's preemptive strikes can push us to "the border of strangeness."

THE BORDER OF STRANGENESS

When life spins out of control, it's like stepping onto an airport terminal automated walkway. We find ourselves moving toward uncertain destinations. One caught up in larger-than-life forces may identify with early American pioneers moving west who, in the midst of trying ordeals, found themselves "at the border of strangeness."[4] All the intimidating things that happened to those wilderness trekkers made them wonder if they would ever feel safe or reach their intended destinations.

We occasionally arrive at a strange border through firmly held, though opposing, viewpoints in the realm of ideas. The search for meaning is difficult in a world debating issues as varied as biomedical ethics, sexual values, race relations, crime and justice, energy alternatives, health care, terrorism, environmental concerns, and interfaces between science and religion.

The late British scholar C. S. Lewis once wrote, "Faith and science form part of a whole. They are intimately related." While that ideal appeals to many scientists and theologians, they have seldom stood on common ground. Diversity marks views of the origin of the universe, the existence of God, and what follows death.

Queens College in Cambridge, England, hosted a rare gathering of 400 astronomers, physicists, biologists, philosophers, and theologians at the third triennial C. S. Lewis Summer Institute. Workshops and lectures focused on the theme: "Cosmos and Creation: Chance or Dance?"

London astrophysicist Christopher Isham said:

Chance refers to the idea that the universe began out of some spontaneous confluction, an unplanned and unmediated occurrence. The dance refers to a scene from Lewis's space trilogy, a beautiful and inspiring description of the biblical origin of the universe and the general meaning of things.[5]

Isham's interpretation of the conference theme reminds us of the limits of scientific solutions to human questions and the need for wisdom that comes from faith.

Strangeness affects more than the world of ideas. Today's navigators face strange borders where dangers lurk. What failsafe shields can prevent the Balkanization of USAmerica like that of former Yugoslavia; halt human rights' violations experienced by China's 1.3 billion citizens; quiet the terror of AIDS infestations in cities such as Bombay and nations such as Zaire; or avoid the terrorist bombing of another World Trade Center, government building, or mosque?

Survival and safety needs have long been recognized as basic to human existence. Yet, gang warfare in Los Angeles one recent year snuffed out more lives than the IRA killed that same period in Northern Ireland. Drive-by shootings are so commonplace in US American cities that citizen vigilante groups have formed to ensure safety. Urban stress syndrome, a newly classified emotional disorder, is common in Chicago, where one is twenty times more likely to get killed than in Northern Ireland.

Living at this "border of strangeness" has caused many persons to lock themselves in to their dwellings in order to keep violence out. Futurist Faith Popcorn has called our attention to "retreat reality," or what others describe as "the cave syndrome." She sees American households digging in.

> Cocooning has people looking for a haven at home—drawing their shades, plumping their pillows, clutching their remotes. Hiding. It is a full-scale retreat into the last controllable (or sort of controllable) environment—your own digs.[6]

A feeling of invasiveness pervades our psychic consciousness. "Out there" people are going to get hurt—whether in public schools, the stock market, labor organizations, toxic faith groups, freeway traffic, big medical centers, or a local shopping mall.

In reaction, Americans are into protecting ourselves as never before. Clues are gun sales and legislation, martial arts and self-care survival lessons, home births, mushrooming enrollments in private schools, and the house church movement. Gated communities are springing up for upscale residents who can afford the price of a protected environment. The sale of home security systems is at an all-time high. Parents look for safe, supervised play sites for their children. Controlling one's environment is a high priority.

We have considered the constancy of change in our lives—from soft transitions, such as aging to harsh realities, such as violence. Choosing a wise course involves calculating the cost. Let's examine some price tags of transition management.

SOME PRICE TAGS OF CHANGE

 TRANSITIONS ARE KEY NUCLEAR EPISODES connecting the otherwise "normal" periods of our lives. Such turning points do not form the whole of life but affect much of our existence.

Life-changing accidents may occur in a moment of time. But the adaptation following a serious accident may alter circumstances, threaten existence, exhaust resources, prompt grief work, and greatly affect one's future. Transitions may take months, even years, before life's turbulence subsides.

Once a person is tracking in a career, enjoying a meaningful relationship, heading toward an objective, or settling into a place, variety may not be the spice of life. Making wise choices, including the best of bad situations, requires real effort, good judgment, and true courage. To remain a pained victim of circumstances is to live trapped and out-of-control.

Calculating the cost of wise change efforts requires action, not mere conjecture. Some price tags of clearheaded changes and choices we must pay include:

Attention to Detail

Attention to detail—along with patient waiting—is required to face and master most challenges. We must discover what is happening to us and act responsibly for ourselves.

I recall a time of intense searching in early marriage for wisdom about a move from one state and one graduate institution to another. It took two years of careful investigation for my wife and me to become convinced that the move was feasible and true to divine guidance. I desired a change, but her inner clock required fine-tuning, gentle persuasion, willingness to uproot our family with a small child, dealing with separation anxiety, and commitment to a larger vision. Our motto was, "Look before you leap" to help determine a wise course of action.

Adaptation and Accommodation

Someone once asked a personal friend how he was adjusting to his wife's sudden death after minor surgery. "You don't expect an amputee to *adjust* quickly to the loss of a limb," he replied. "He has to *adapt* to a different existence. And that's true of me." Change, whether gradual or hasty, forces us to adapt to new circumstances. We call that adaptive process *transition*.

When the Union of Soviet Socialist Republics responded to Mikhail Gorbachev's *perestroika* (economic restructuring) and *glasnost* (openness) vision, the union collapsed into numerous new/old republics. The Commonwealth of Independent States exists no longer as one but many. Revisioning the military, political, economic, and social environments of those new nations has been painfully disruptive for millions of Russian people. It may require decades to negotiate that metamorphosis.

Accommodation takes time and the courage to endure. A company declares bankruptcy and terminates hundreds of employees. A family moves from Silicon Valley to Colorado Springs because of dad's or mom's new job opportunity. Aging happens—silent as spring or with the onset of aches, pains, and losses. A multinational corporation faces major opposition to its overseas capitalistic initiatives from "tribalistic" rivals. Adjustments to such alterations in our lives do not come without anger, confusion, and persistence.

Ambiguity

People facing new circumstances respond in dissimilar, unique fashion. One person's meat is another's poison, goes the old maxim. Jack Mitchell's taking a promotion required his family to move at the beginning of his son's senior year in high school. Tad was elected cheerleader for team sports for that crucial final year. The move violated his selfhood, took him from all his friends, and sank his self-esteem. Only after Tad's complete emotional collapse and psychiatric hospitalization did his father confess: "It was the most expensive promotion of my life."

In an election, a candidate for political office wins, but three public-minded office seekers lose. An executive is terminated in a company takeover. Power brokers may have won, but a family may have been destroyed in the process. Personnel shifts may introduce new blood into an organization, but hundreds of lives may be stressed in the ensuing chaos.

Ambiguous situations are confusing, even angering. Finally, somebody has to choose so life can move on.

Decision Time

Transitions are decision times. There is often a dyadic quality to a life event. Things could go one way or another way. The modification process is unpredictable.

As the Peoples Republic of China incorporates Hong Kong, thousands of that former British crown colony's residents will emigrate. Given the solidarity of Chinese families, when one member of a household leaves, the extended family faces a decision. "Should we stay here near the Wongs? Or should we move with Tan to Vancouver?"

When we open one decisive door, a dozen new doors may open before us. A visionary experience (for example, a divine calling), a temptation, a career opportunity, a purchase, an illness, or a critical incident—each requires decision and action. A delay could be a life or death matter. Some interruptions provoke feelings of helplessness.

Loss of Control

Loss of control of one's physical well-being, environment, family ties, vocation, financial status, location—even one's destiny—marks many transitions. The biological clock, for example, says it is time for preteen Justin or Joanne to enter middle school. Time forces a child to leave the (hopefully) safe haven of childhood for the hormonal changes and risky chances of adolescence. One moves up the educational ladder to a higher grade but down the status ladder among older students. His or her social clock may spin out of control, marred by timidity or loneliness, and affect adversely learning skills.[7]

When control of events, resources, or circumstances is lost, life is thrown off balance. One's sense of well-being is shaken by uncertainties. One's reliance on "the system" and social interconnections are jolted out of the ordinary.

When an orthopedic surgeon revealed his HIV positive diagnosis, he was terminated immediately by two medical centers. Hundreds of his former patients may have been placed at risk through invasive surgeries he had performed. Because of his delayed self-revelation, other lives have been endangered. He has since been diagnosed with AIDS. Life requires a plot, not just a plight, for the future.

Accountability

Fortunately, we are shapers of life's story, not merely its passive victims. A family journal advertisement pictures the maturing young adult's growing sense of accountability:

Leaving home was all you thought about. Europe. Oregon. The other side of town. . . . it didn't matter. You ventured. You landed, you took off again. When the road ran out, you took on capitalism. A real job. A spouse. Now you're selecting things for the *family* room.

The point? You can't run away from responsibilities forever. Adulthood awaits, though some authorities hold that true adulthood does not begin until the age-thirty transition.

There is another side to accountability. You need forgiveness and support when you "blow it." A visitor recalled his conversation with the postmaster of a Southern town.

"You see that house?" Red Neill said, pointing down the hill. "An alcoholic widow lives there with her two children. She's a smart schoolteacher, but the community doesn't think much of her. Mickey started drinking after her husband died. Seems like people don't want to understand her or try to help her. (He paused.) What this town needs to learn is the power of forgiveness!"

Was Mickey not responsible? Yes, she was accountable for her actions. Life had shortchanged her; she paid it back trying to escape. Her alcoholism was not harmless; neither was the community's judgmentalism. Perhaps no one was to blame, but all were responsible.

Events can isolate us. We need people to count on along the way. Such friendships should be forged *before* crises arise.

People to Count On

Lillian was a late middle-age member of a small congregation. She and her deacon husband had their family. But to their surprise, an unplanned pregnancy occurred. Lil felt she was beyond menopause, but nature tricked her. Then it mocked her.

Becky was born a Downs syndrome child. Lillian took it as punishment from God for not wanting another baby. She wisely turned to her sensitive husband and older children, as well as to members of her faith community, for understanding and stability. They shared her pained decision to raise Becky at home rather than institutionalize her.

When a person is thrown off balance, people who care are important. The twelve-step program of A.A. would not amount to much without support groups.[8] American novelist James Street, author of *The Gauntlet*, once shared his family's story with a class of university students. Street described his wife's alcoholism and stated how crucial the Alcoholics Anonymous group meetings were to her sobriety. He had no moral inhibitions about the use of alcohol, he said. But at their house, alcohol was out because of his spouse's unhealthy addiction.

Given extended life expectancy, along with its reversals, many navigators find themselves starting aspects of life again.

Starting Over

Saying goodbye to one's status, locale, work assignment, or group of friends has its own bittersweetness. Saying hello to a new life phase, job opportunity, or predicament presents us with unique challenges. New beginnings force us to examine our core values, unload non-essential baggage, watch our pathway, narrow our focus, deal with changing expectations, even learn a new language if one becomes an expatriate.

Laura, recently widowed, moved from her sizeable residence into a nearby retirement community. In describing her anxiety to a friend, she confessed: "I have never spent a night alone in my entire life." Trying to begin again, Laura felt out of sync in her retirement center apartment.

Petrified with fear, despite a security alarm system, she returned to her former home for a couple of days. But Laura was fearful and missed Sam terribly, so she returned to Coast Point Retirement Village. Unable to settle into the "old folks" community, she had all the locks changed on the doors at her big house and returned home to live alone. Her panic attacks lasted several months. Laura found that beginning again as a single, senior adult is hard.

Starting over may prompt a burst of creativity, especially if one has gotten an unfavorable health report. Award-winning composer Henry Mancini died at age seventy of liver and pancreatic cancer. Mancini's music formed the soundtrack of a generation. He pioneered in using different elements of American music when creating film scores. His family surrounded Mancini with attentiveness and affection as the cancer intensified its grip.[9] The winner of four Oscars and twenty Grammy Awards, Mancini composed at the piano until shortly before his death.

Faith, Courage, and Acceptance

Coming to terms with change can push us into an uncertain state between despair and hope. Historians recall President Lyndon Baines Johnson's admission to former colleagues of the U.S. House of representatives and Senate following John F. Kennedy's assassination in November, 1963.

Johnson confessed in essence, "All I own or have ever possessed I would give *not* to be standing here at this moment." It was an agonizing, abrupt, anguished switch of presidential leadership. Taking the reigns of governance required confidence, courage, and commitment to major responsibilities. The record of his civil rights legislation and dream of a Great Society (despite the war in Vietnam) speaks for itself.

In less notable, though no less remarkable, ways, transitions prompt us to trust God as the true foundation for life. Ben C. Ollenburger relates the story behind J. Christian Beker's testament of faith and courage during World War II.[10] In his foreword to Beker's classic study of the problem of evil, he describes the dehumanizing conditions Beker endured as a slave laborer during the Nazi occupation of the Netherlands. Beker's terrible experiences shaped his view of suffering and hope.

Beker told his story of tornness between belief and unbelief in tandem with biblical stories. The Scriptures reflect the paradox of humankind's trust in a good creator alongside the fact of immense pain and human evil (Rom 8:28). In calculating the cost of change, openness to the future is crucial.

Vision and Initiative

My wife and I once visited the remote Peruvian city of Cuzco, high in the Andes mountains, enroute to the fabled ruins of the Inca empire, Machu Picchu. The native Indians of Cuzco told us the name means "navel of the world." Their ancient tribal forebears imagined life for all humankind originated in that southeastern Peruvian valley.

You may know people facing change who are like those convinced Peruvians. They act and talk as if the world is limited to their experience. They are frozen in time.

Transitions compel new initiatives, based on realistic vision of life's circumstances, plus available resources. Revisioning the future has significant power to change one's attitudes and actions in the present. Upon completing formal education, ideally one enters the world of work. There may be delays or detours. By thirty-something, a single person may find a mate. By forty, a couple may have a son or daughter. At sixty, a person may become a grandparent for the first time. One lives out one's days futureward, in hope, not in chronic depression, drug or alcohol addiction, sexual escapades, or goalless existence.

Many of life's challenges and choices are elective. On the other hand, some problems become permanent. An abusive spouse is intransigent. A wound will not heal. An anxiety will not go away. Job opportunities do not turn up. Singleness stays and sexual frustration deepens. A severely handicapped or challenged family member must be cared for. A fatal diagnosis must be faced. Evil events happen. Such permanent predicaments seem to require greater faith than life's sunny days. And the content and nature of your faith are subject to change over time.

In summary, we have considered some ways life changes—from quiet mutations of the aging process to violence in contemporary societies. We have shared stories to live by, not mere abstractions. Rather than viewing transitions with sadness and lament, change has been pictured as a spur to move us forward, as a challenge, a tonic, as a call to care. There are times and places to grieve over life's deficits, as well as occasions for bright balloons and celebrations. With this in mind, we examine the many sides of change.

REFLECTIVE EXERCISES

For Thought:

1. What are some changes you anticipated this year that have been accomplished? What life goals have not yet been achieved?

2. With threats all around, have you found yourself "cocooning," looking for a safe haven, or trying to avoid change? In what ways?

3. What price tags of change are too high for you to pay? Example: Loss of control.

4. If you had one trusted person with whom to share life's change-points or to help relieve anxiety, who would that person be? Why?

For Discussion:

1. In reflecting on stories of lifechange thus far, how does one's age or generational outlook affect change management?

2. If your physician determined that a quiet change, such as cancer, was occurring in your body, what responses would be appropriate?

3. In what ways do you see persons caught up in larger-than-life forces and moving toward uncertain destinations? Are such occurrences having positive or negative effects in your own life? Your family? Your church or synagogue?

4. How do transitions compel us to take new initiatives in life? Can you illustrate such an initiative in your own experience?

5. Suggest some ways our homes can prepare family members for responsible citizenship in a changing, pluralistic society.

NOTES

[1]William Bridges, *Transitions: Making Sense of Life's Changes* (Reading MA: Addison-Wesley, 1980) 45.

[2]Ellen Chang, "Hits Come Early to Boy of Summer," *Fort Worth Star-Telegram*, 21 May 1994, 1A, 36.

[3]As reported in the *Baptist Message*, 19 May 1994, 8.

[4]Attributed to American writer Wallace Stegner, author of *The American West as Living Space* (Ann Arbor MI: University of Michigan Press, 1987) and numerous stories of the old West.

[5]Christopher Isham, quoted in Jo Kadlecek, "Science Gets Religion," *Christianity Today*, 12 September 1994, 58-59.

[6]Faith Popcorn, *The Popcorn Report: Faith Popcorn on the Future of Your Company, Your World, Your Life* (New York: Doubleday, 1991) 27.

[7]See Daniel Goleman, *Emotional Intelligence* (New York: Bantam Books, 1995) 214-24.

[8]Robert Wuthnow, *Sharing the Journey: Support Groups and America's New Quest for Community* (New York: Lexington Books, 1994).

[9]Hugh Downs and Barbara Walters, ABC-TV, 20/20, 27 May 1994; "Henry Mancini Dead at Age 70," *The Daily Sentinel*, Grand Junction CO, 15 June 1994, 9A.

[10]J. Christian Beker, *Suffering & Hope: The Biblical Vision and the Human Predicament* (Grand Rapids MI: Eerdmans, 1994).

Chapter 2

THE MANY
SIDES OF CHANGE

Stories of the American frontier, of people pushing bravely westward from the Atlantic to the Pacific coast, are a centerpiece of New World history. The French observer Alexis de Tocqueville wrote in his diary in 1831: "The American has no time to tie himself to anything, he grows accustomed only to change, and . . . (regards) it as the natural state of man."[1] Museums along the Oregon trail and California and Alaska gold rush treks showcase memorabilia of people, animals, weapons, tools, clothing, and means of travel early pioneers used in pursuit of new frontiers.

Because life cycles through seasons, we pursue new frontiers of meaning, creative energy for work and leisure and self-transcendence in each passage. *Passage* is more than just another buzzword. It suggests we are on a spiritual journey. We are in time as fish are in water. Like a child viewing colored shapes through a kaleidoscope, we encounter variations in life's passages. True, some things don't change. They are like granite. Others that run as deep as life itself, such as one's attitudes and values, may prove malleable.

Perhaps you are wondering what things will endure and what changepoints may be anticipated for you and persons you cherish. Consider the wisdom of two trusted pathfinders.

THE PATHFINDERS' LEGACY

Catholic mystics have seldom confined their faith to cloistered walls. Their influence has inspired spiritual endeavor in many nations. Mother Teresa reached into Calcutta's slums and squalor, and beyond. The late Catholic seer Thomas Merton viewed spiritual sensitivity, not as an escape from the common life, but as a way of sharing in the redemption of the world. The true prophet, he said in Bangkok on the day he died, "is essentially someone who takes up a critical attitude towards the contemporary world and its structures."[2]

Mother Teresa would have appreciated Merton's comparison of the prophetic role in society of poets and caregivers. At a meeting of Latin American poets in Mexico City in 1964, Merton said both poets and seers reject the political art of setting man against man and the commercial practice of setting a price on persons. Mother Teresa has stayed busy doing the Lord's work. She has noted, "Today it is very fashionable to talk about the poor. Unfortunately, it is not fashionable to talk with them."[3]

Seers such as Merton and Teresa invite modern pathfinders to seek God's shaping hand in facing life's experiences. Merton said the true life-changer is a contemplative "person . . . who withdraws deliberately to the margin of society with a view to deepening fundamental human experience." In one's closeness to God, he or she transcends marginality. A person with a vision of eternal values "pushes to the very frontiers of human experience and strives to go beyond, to find out what transcends the ordinary level of existence."[4]

It is this going-beyondness of spiritual qualities—for instance, faith, hope, discernment, and love that propels us onward. True believers hold that God does not leave us to face life's callings and challenges alone.

PERMANENT AND PASSING THINGS

 THE MANY SIDES OF CHANGE GENERATE PARADIGM SHIFTS all about us. Old assumptions are giving way to new ways of thinking, revised value systems, new means of communication, new rules of competition, and new products and services.

Several years had passed since my last visit to Hong Kong, and the dynamics of economic changes could actually be felt as well as seen. Smartly dressed executives passed us in chauffer-driven limousines; Western-attired office workers hastened to keep appointments; construction cranes arched steel loads skyward; and hundreds of pedestrians talked on cellular phones as they walked crowded streets. The linkage of West and East could be measured in volume of customers at McDonald's and the Colonel's Kentucky Fried Chicken restaurants; CNN telecasts of Pacific Rim news (with inserted items from around the globe); popular

USAmerican ballads in hotel lobbies; and popularity of the international cafe chain Planet Hollywood.

No doubt about image exports of big name brands of clothing, cigarettes, soft drinks, and electronic gadgets. The logos, brand names, movie stars, and advertising slogans of New York, Seattle, and Los Angeles belong to Hong Kong, Tokyo, Rio de Janeiro, and Mexico City. Athletic shoes and sporting goods, shopping malls and theme parks, video, theater, books, and music are all part of planet Earth's expanding marketplace.

The lives of ordinary people are being reshaped by globalization of the economy. The expansion of multinational companies beyond all national boundaries clashes with local cultures, governments, and tribal protectionism. In past eras, processes of industrialization—financial empires, assembly line production, oil, steel transportation of goods—gained sovereignty in developed nations. Government antitrust regulation was required to bridle greed's threats to USAmerican society.

Today, billions of dollars are spent in advertising and in expanding spheres of influence by global corporations. Political scientist Benjamin Barber reminds us of how globalism and tribalistic resistance are reshaping our world. Today's entrepreneurs, he says, are far more powerful than nineteenth-century industrialists. Their global control of ideas, information, news, entertainment, and advertising struggles to shape "the very sinews of our postmodern soul."[5]

Persons who read Barber's *Jihad vs. McWorld* will sense his profound concern for democracy in a world of competing economic and social forces. "Jihad" is a metaphor for all the world's "narrowly conceived faiths" aligned against "every kind of interdependence . . . cooperation and mutuality . . . against modernity itself as well as the future in which modernity issues."[6] On the other hand, "McWorld" is Barber's metaphor for all the multinational enterprises that capitalize on earth's longing for possessions, that see humankind as a gigantic marketplace.

Could this be the era of a new breed of pathfinder, caught between Babel and Disneyland, who refuse to cower before tribal sniper fire and to knuckle under to icons such as Coca Cola, KFC, and Adidas? It is quite possible, however unconsciously, that we are each, in our own way, becoming citizens of earth.[7] Students from many lands are exchanging campuses, business travelers are learning new languages, and U.S. troops socialize overseas with strangers from many shores. Ideas, belief systems, virtues, and, conversely, all kinds of evils, flow the Internet. Indeed, we need a chart and compass to navigate the terrain ahead.

THREE WORDS FOR BUILDING A FUTURE

 IF YOU ARE LIKE THE AVERAGE "JANE" OR "JOE," you desire a framework of meaning to help you chart the passages of your change-filled existence.

We try to name experience and cope with events happening around and inside us. Here are three words for building your future:

Prompter *(defining moment)*

Lessons from survivors of change reveal that transitions in one's life course have antecedents. They are triggered by defining moments I call prompters. The causative event may be a ringing wake-up call, for example, an accident. The prompter may be unconscious—denied, or out of awareness. Such may be true for the Korean youth in a pre-medical program at the University of Chicago. Seung's father is a physician. His family expects him to excel in medicine. Privately, Seung prefers oceanography and may flunk out of pre-med in order to avoid losing face later on as a failed physician.

Prompters are more than rhetoric. Like a near-death experience, once a person survives a critical event, the effects have lasting results.

Passage *(adaptation)*

The work of transition, whether planned or spontaneous, propels a person, family, or larger system onto a journey of adaptation. Such a passage evolves through a series of phases, often designated as "seasons" of one's life. In institutions, change may be detailed as a transition management plan. Such alterations are seldom straight lines, for they are emotionally twisted and complex. The patterning of specific events is often a spiral—with attempts at resolution, searches for a new pathway, and efforts to leave the past behind.

Process (*resolution or readaptation*)

If one's attempts at resolution go well, we view the outcome as "success" or "stability." Life begins to feel "normal." Such a consequence of change may be viewed as reinventing relationships or finding one's way or gaining the freedom to move ahead with life. Of course, the process might end disastrously in a series of violent, aberrant, or maladaptive behaviors. Change becomes a harbinger for our future story. It signifies that life is process, moving toward future goals.

HOW CHANGE HAPPENS

Let us examine some typical causes (prompters) of new beginnings, since all passages are not the same. The most subtle forms of change advance quietly with *chronology*—transformations imposed by the passing of time. The movement of history's clock appears relentless. We are young, pursue vocations, develop religious loyalties, marry and rear children, or elect to remain single. We become mid-careerists, then golden-aged retirees—all in the twinkling of an eye, it seems.[8]

Choices dictate many changes in our lives: to live here and *Choices* not there, to divorce rather than remain married, to serve in the military rather than civilian life, to vacation at the Grand Canyon rather than at Disney World, to restructure a corporation rather than terminate jobs, to vote Democrat rather than Republican, to commute to work rather than move, or to seek to overthrow a corrupt government rather than remain its victim.

What serves as choice for one person may force change by *circum-* *circumstances* upon others. For example, a disturbed ex-attorney *stances* gunned down two Texas court jurists and wounded three other *of* persons in a grudge slaying.[9] Spouses of the slain men became *choice* instant widows, with small children to care for and educate. Law enforcement officials ordered metal detectors for all entry points at the county courthouse. And a one-time attorney was sentenced to a term in prison.

Choices and circumstances interact as people face transitions. A famine in Ethiopia (circumstance), for instance, may prompt economic aide (choice) from Sweden. A civil war in any country of the world may force U.N. action with an international peacekeeping force.

Crises are carriers of change: a destructive earthquake, an airliner explosion and crash, war smoldering in the Middle East, an ominous diagnosis of cancer or AIDS, a fatal auto accident, or involuntary termination of one's job. Some crises come through silent developmental processes—like puberty or menopause. Others, like a hurricane, rage violently, destroy property worth fortunes, and throw life off balance.

Two Chinese characters picturing the dyadic nature of crisis appear together—*danger* and *opportunity*. A personal crisis may follow an attack upon one's character, or criticism of one's art, or conflict over one's position on a key issue. A crisis may arise from a financial bonanza, for instance, winning a PGA golf tournament; or critical loss, for example, Japan's humiliation following defeat in World War II.

For an Argentine soccer star, a crisis came when he tested positive for five banned substances and was expelled from the World Cup games.[10] Until then, the thirty-three-year-old Diego Maradona was regarded as the world's best player.

Convictions growing out of visionary experiences or deeply held persuasions may thrust a person into new directions. Alexander Solzhenitsyn, you may recall, felt compelled to expose certain vices of the former Soviet Communist party system. Solzhenitsyn was expelled from Russia after his outlawed book about Soviet concentration camps, *The Gulag Archipelago*, was published in the West. He had spent eight years in the camps, after World War II, for criticizing Josef Stalin.

In 1994, the Nobel laureate returned to his homeland after twenty years of exile. He was greeted in Valdivostok by thousands of admirers, a host of reporters, and a telegram from then president Boris Yelstin saying his talent and experience "will help us in rebuilding Russia." Dissent took Solzhenitsyn on a long journey. Time will tell whether he can actually go home again.

Religious conversion may prompt profound change in one's character and life direction. Faith in God may take persons on long journeys, for example, the Apostle Paul's missional experiences following his Christian conversion. When religion gets sick, on the other hand, deeply held persuasions may become delusions, leading a person to violent behavior or despair. With God's help, internal work may reconnect a person with a long forgotten dream or help someone honor a commitment. True conversion touches all aspects of life.

Cultural (or historic) shifts motivate some persons to interact with changing events and seize fresh opportunities. Today's woman may select military service or high political office as a career, for example, and observers give it no thought. The social fabric has stretched under new pressures.

More than thirty million abortions have been performed on American women in the decades since the Supreme Court's *Roe vs. Wade* decision. Now, Norma McCorvey, the "Jane Roe" at the center of the Supreme Court's 1973 landmark ruling that legalized abortion, has become a Christian. She wants out of the nightmare of her past shame and guilt. Abortion rights activists, new abortion methods such as the controversial pill RU-486, as well as right-to-life advocates continue to influence our respect (or lack of regard) for human life.

Corrective or reconstructive changes affect our lives in healing and freeing ways. Persons affected by stage fright, for example, overcome in group psychotherapy sessions the adverse effects of early childhood experiences of crushing shame, scolding, and degrading disparagement by parents. A child disfigured in an accidental home fire learns to face the future with optimism following months of tissue transplants and reconstructive cosmetic surgery. An abusive spouse hears his wife's woundedness for the first time through family systems therapy sessions. Times such as these are breakthroughs, when we are able to face vocational demands or relational expectations with renewed strength.

A passage you are experiencing right now may be confusing as you are thrust into an in-between state. Like an astronaut, weightless in space, you may lose your sense of direction in a career change. Confusion marks the lives of almost one million US American executives who, according to the Bureau of Labor Statistics, have lost their jobs in recent years through corporate reorganizations.

Change, journey, and outcome (process) is the normal rhythm of life's transitions.[11] An outcome is seldom the spot one occupied before. Rather, it is the path to survival—the, "Aha! I can make it!" assurance when one is moving forward with life again. We call such mid-course corrections or adjustments "finding a balance." In medicine it is called homeostasis or wellness. For believers, the process becomes spiritual renewal.

Life at its best faces compromises and tradeoffs. You may have to settle for less-than-ideal outcomes in one instance; yet, feel blessed in another set of circumstances.

All of life is a process of anticipation, disorientation, and struggle for reorientation on the pathway of growth. Change is more than "nature's way" in seasonal fashion. It is the course of life of which the Bible speaks: "Let us run with perseverance the race marked out for us" (Heb 12:1b, NIV). Next, we shall see that charting life's course requires acquaintance with transition themes.

REFLECTIVE EXERCISES

For Thought:

1. In the past twelve months, the following events outside my control have directly affected my life (e.g., work, the economy, health):

2. How might a private, contemplative person, such as Thomas Merton, affect fundamental human experience in the social order?

3. What difference has religious faith made in a loss I experienced this past year? (e.g., divorce, victim of theft, job loss).

4. My dreams for my family (or company or organization) have not panned out as I had hoped (e.g., promotion, merger plan). So here is what I am doing about life's circumstances:

5. In my own search for meaning, I have decided to (e.g., read a book, join a group):

For Discussion:

1. What difference does it make to have a community of kindred spirits with whom to share changes and challenges in life?

2. With new ways of thinking and cultural expression going on, what are some of the "new values" taking shape around us?

3. In what ways have you noticed church or denomination-switching among your acquaintances? Does marriage cause new partners to change religious affiliation?

4. How may turning points or forks in the road trip people up in day-to-day relationships?

5. How might a person's sense of partnership with/connectedness to God strengthen him or her for life's vocation?

NOTES

[1]Alexis de Tocqueville, quoted in G. W. Pierson, *Tocqueville and Beaumont in America* (New York: Oxford University Press, 1938) 119.

[2]Thomas Merton, quoted in Naomi B. Stone, et al., eds., *The Asian Journal of Thomas Merton* (New York: New Directions, 1973) 329.

[3]Mother Teresa, *Mother Teresa: In My Own Words*, comp. Jose Luis Gonzalez-Baldo (Liguori MO: Liguori Publications, 1996).

[4]Thomas Merton, *Thomas Merton, Monk: A Monastic Tribute* Patrick Hart, ed. (New York: Sheed and Ward, Inc., 1974) 53, 135, 183.

[5]Benjamin R. Barber, *Jihad vs. McWorld* (New York: Ballentine Books, 1996) 298.

[6]Ibid., 4-20.

[7]Nine million USAmericans were said to have toured Europe and Britain in the summer of 1996. Multiply that by tens of thousands of US troops, business travelers, and foreign exchange students to gain a perspective of our involvements in the worldwide web of life.

[8]See, for example, Gail Sheehy, *New Passages: Mapping Your Life Across Time* (New York: Random House, 1995). Longitudinal studies by Daniel J. Levinson and a research team at Yale University School of Medicine revealed universal sequences of development during five eras of the adult life span. See *The Seasons of a Man's Life* (New York: Alfred A. Knopf, 1978). Their studies of the lives of forty men over time disclosed stable epochs in each of the five eras, lasting about six to eight years; and transition periods between stable times of about four to five years. Levinson's studies picture the discontinuity of development from one era to another, with much emotional work required in transitions as well as periods of stability.

[9]Ernie Makovy, "Tarrant Courthouse Gunman Kills 2, Wounds 3," *Fort Worth Star-Telegram*, 12 July 1992, A-1.

[10]Steve Davis, "Maradona Kicked out of World Cup," *The Dallas Morning News*, 1 July 1994, B-1, 5.

[11]John Kotre and Elizabeth Hall, *Seasons of Life: Our Dramatic Journey from Birth to Death* (Boston: Little, Brown, & Co., 1990);

Richard O. Straub, *Seasons of Life Study Guide* (New York: Worth Publishers, Inc., 1990); Paul B. Baltes and Orville G. Brim, Jrs., eds., *Life Span Development and Behavior*, vol. 2 (New York: Academic Press, 1979).

Chapter 3

WHEN THINGS
ARE SET IN MOTION

You can count on it. New situations force us into choice points at the most surprising, sometimes inopportune, times. Attention-getting experiences, such as a wind-shear incident after takeoff of a passenger plane, churn our emotions, preoccupy our minds, drain our energies, and force us to learn more about the business of living. When we are stretched by some wake-up call, we may think only survival counts, not the destination. But both the *way* we go through shattering events and the *goal* we reach matter.

When facing a new challenge, obstacle, or conflict, our temptation is to react as we have always done in the past. Reacting is easier than responding with a new strategy or fresh resolve. The Japanese have a word for endurance from the code of the samuri: *gaman*. It means "to bear the unbearable," to endure losses without complaint. Steering a course through a stressful situation requires more ingenuity and determination than endurance alone.

When things are set in motion by change, we are faced with new choice points. Life forces us to decide and act. It refuses to take "no comment" for an answer. We are products of our choices within life's circumstances, not mere victims. Just as a small pilot boat guides a large ship through harbor traffic and danger to the sea, we need points on our compass to help us face and resolve circumstances rather than being mere victims. We need help now!

 LET'S EXPLORE:
- What turning points are you facing at this moment?
- Are you in danger of repeating old response patterns? ✖
- Will someone rescue you, or must you work it out?

- When you decided before, were you a victim, a martyr, or an achiever?
- What are you complaining about that will not change?
- What will happen if you do not work things out?
- What better thing can happen if you do work on it?

I NEED HELP RIGHT NOW!

At the outset, I mentioned some peak mapmakers—Gandhi, Merton, Bonhoffer, Keller, and Mother Teresa—whose change strategies made them real pathfinders. What behaviors did they practice that are clear and transferable into our own survival skills?

Clues for facing choice points come, not just from those noted navigators, but also from ordinary people. Here are some strategies wise persons have used to face life's defining moments:

- commitment to a worthy goal with high purpose as a mission
- guided by principles of integrity and worthwhile priorities
- desire to empower themselves and others for creative living
- reflect a capacity for self-transformation through courage, endurance, and lifelong learning
- ability to face and overcome obstacles despite discouragement
- can face life's adversities with faith and flexibility
- view attention-getters, detours, and challenges with possibility thinking toward creative alternatives
- desire to make a worthwhile contribution—a true difference—to their generation
- know how to use straight talk for clear communication
- willing to forgive when offending parties show genuine repentance and desire for restoration
- possess the spiritual power to see life through no matter what change or crisis comes
- willing to learn from their own mistakes, make mid-course corrections, and move on with a hopeful attitude
- function appropriately in intimate relationships, without faltering over issues of gender, ethnicity, power, or generational differences
- practice self-care—physically, emotionally, and spiritually—in an effort to stay well
- envision the "long look" at life to see outcomes, beyond passages and change processes

Learning how to use these compass points is soulwork. Here, I am using *soul* in the classic sense of one's true self—the vital essence of being human. Persons pursuing soulwork view life's passages as spiritual journeying, not as some cosmic dead end. Soul, here, refers to our center of focus, our vitality of being, and our connection with God. Soulwork is some of the most important work we can do.[1]

When things are set in motion, it is not possible to see the heavy traffic, road hazards, or vistas just ahead. The distance from here to there may be moving from preadolescence to the new territory of puberty. Or it might be space travelers launched in NASA's ill-fated shuttle *Challenger*, flying to their deaths. Sometimes, O-rings fail. Life may press us through changes of such magnitude and mystery that there are more lessons to learn and more sacrifices to make than we can handle. Again, life may offer us such traveling companions, understanding support, wise mentorship, and dependable resources that changes are negotiated with relative ease.

It is to transition themes that we turn for wisdom and guidance. What is it like to face a crossing and pass over to the other side? Youths pushing hard toward adulthood may claim to have no "clue" as to what's happening in their lives. Still, kids facing pressures from peers and social changes need clues to get there from here.

KIDS NEED CLUES TO RISKS AND RESPONSIBILITIES

When I was seventeen, having finished high school and one year of college, an urge stirred inside me to explore the larger world. By then, I had traveled as far north from my Louisiana home as Niagara Falls in Ontario, Canada, and had explored the wonders of government buildings in Washington, D. C. I had had student work experiences as a hardware store clerk, as an office employee for a national bus company, and as a disc jockey for an NBC-affiliate radio station. Though my family could not afford tuition in the Ivy League, I had been accepted into Harvard College in Cambridge, Massachusetts, as well.

It was wartime in Europe. My freedom might become terminal if I were drafted into military service, or so I thought. My need to experience L-I-F-E was a not-so-silent struggle toward manhood and independence from hearth and home. At seventeen, all things appear possible; adolescents imagine they are invincible. Thus, I set out to discover the world.

My journey took me to Plaquemine, Louisiana, a small town southwest of Baton Rouge, on the Mississippi River. As luck would have it, I met a middle-aged ex-prisoner who had recently been discharged from the Louisiana state penitentiary at Angola. Jim West had served a seven year sentence for murdering a man who had raped his niece. Each year in prison had etched itself into his hardened face.

Because he took a liking to me, Jim arranged an introduction with Captain Bill Truxillo of the river tugboat, *Sweet William*, on which West worked as a cook. They needed a deckhand; I needed a job in order to support my world travels. There was a bunk for me aboard the neat workhorse vessel, tasks to perform, and a place at the mess table at mealtime.

The *Sweet William* plied the Intracoastal Waterway as far west as oil storage tanks on Galveston Bay, then pushed oil barges back east to processing plants along the Mississippi River. Our route took us through Acadian country in Southwest Louisiana, across the Sabine Lake, then onto the Texas coast and back again. I did not see much of "the world" but did make some important discoveries.

Personal experiences aboard the *Sweet William* were far more than adventure travels. They were leaving home, self-forming, demanding happenings. There was life with the crew in limited physical space. After work, there was time for quiet reflection, soul searching, new respect for family (back home) ties, and appreciation for the rough and tumble "real world."

In due course, I left the tugboat and life on the Mississippi River, but lessons learned aboard the *Sweet William* did not leave me. Though I was a greenhorn on the crew, the men respected me. I did a man's work and drew a man's pay. I suffered loneliness unlike any pain I had ever known. My values set boundaries for behavior different from that of my companions. In that mobile workplace, I experienced my own uniqueness from "the others"— not alienation—but distinct identity. By the time I returned home, something crucial had been accomplished. While I respected home ties and family traditions, relationships severed that seventeenth summer would never be the same. I knew that I must find my own way in the world. ✓✓ Yes

FINDING ONE'S OWN WAY

A pilgrimage like that described here is a bridge experience from one life epoch to another. Uprootedness is normal in mid-adolescence. One lets go of reliable care providers at home and strikes out on a search for "the others" who may give acceptance and who will confirm his or her identity. The late Erik H. Erikson called this taking leave of one's safe hold on adolescence and searching for a firm grasp on adulthood a "psychosocial moratorium." It had been his own experience as a youth abandoned by his father when he wandered as an artist around Europe.

The word *psychosocial* took on special meaning for Erikson. It bridged "the so-called 'biological' formulations of psycho-analysis and newer ones which take the cultural environment into more systematic consideration."[2] And *moratorium* implied a time-between-the-times, when full adult risks and responsibilities awaited, but were not socially imposed. One makes a youthful decision to leave or is expelled or is pushed out of home. But one's faith-craft is untested. If torn from one's moorings too early, a person experiences trauma, inadequacy, and uncertainty. One fears failure and keeps trying to make up for leaving home too early. Thus, such leave-taking may be for better or worse.

Family therapist Murray Bowen, of the Georgetown University Medical School, called finding one's way "the differentiation of the self."[3] One bears a family name, has roots in a particular culture, knows the stories, and lives with a genetic heritage. Each of us seeks confirmation of our unique identity—blessing from significant others and from our creator.

Finding one's way (identity formation) cannot be forced or rushed. Society, in Erikson's view, should grant youthful novices a period of delay from adult obligations. The delay is more than a gap in one's developmental history. Used well, the delay grants a young person a period of experimentation, ritualization, playfulness, and tentative commitments before settling down. Experiments are highly varied—from travel to study, from military service to apprenticeships. For deeply troubled young adults, the vision-quest may take on destructive behavior patterns with most serious consequences.

Youthful pilgrimages provide a new worldview, highlight vocational themes, challenge our assumptions, lay bare our souls, and pull us toward the mystery of faith. Short excursions early on permit us to find our strengths and limits; also, to test the seaworthiness of our "faith-craft" for the great oceans beyond. In my own case, I went on to serve as a ship's officer during World War II. Vision-quests furnish the groundwork for human learning and growth from experience. They provide essential linkage from one passage to another. Such exploratory events are filled with complexity, risk, improbability, and promise.

As we move through time, it is not easy to locate or leave what the late Swedish U.N. secretary general Dag Hammarskjold called "markings." Trustworthy mapmakers blazed their trails so that persons who followed could find their way.

> ✳ IN AN EFFORT TO "MARK TRAIL," I shall emphasize some ways to tell time and to discover what time it is in our lives.

LEARNING TO TELL TIME

More than 3,000 years ago, a wise person prayed to his God: "Teach us to count our days that we may gain a wise heart" (Ps 90:12). Thoughtful persons have sought to use time well in order to reach the full measure of wisdom life intends. How does one tell time in an era of computer savvy and multimedia, interactive technology?

Researchers speak of three clocks that move throughout the life span. The clock metaphors offer us a way to mark time in our own life story, as well as in history. They help us to name and number our days in the social order.

Biological clock is a metaphor describing one's physical development. It times birth, growth, health, illness, aging, and death. The term *social clock* reflects society's age norms for when certain life events should occur. Age-linked developmental tasks include: readiness for and entering school, cognitive and emotional growth, managing sexuality, relational skills, getting married, starting a family, beginning a vocation, job change or loss, and retirement. In *New Passages*, Gail Sheehy illuminates disparities in viewing the life cycle, but argues that "important aspects of our inner development remain true to stage."[4]

Psychological clock symbolizes your sense of selfhood and meaningful connections with all other persons on life's journey.[5] The psyche or self determines gender uniqueness, establishes identity, measures itself against other persons, strives toward goals, endures ambiguity and pain, survives conflicts and losses, tolerates traumatic events, and points one toward wholeness. The ancient psalmist called his goal "an undivided heart" (Ps 86: 11-13). We call it maturity.

In addition to these means for describing life-cycle time, we should add the *spiritual clock*. We have a space in the self into which only God can fit. It is our capacity for faith and religious experience. The spiritual clock times the ultimate sweep of our hopeful imagination; our reaches beyond mystery for a dependable life structure; our longing for a center to anchor life's deepest loyalties; and for meaningful connections for our commitments, love, and will.

 THE SPIRITUAL CLOCK MEASURES ONE'S SEARCH FOR MEANING, relational skills, maturity, struggle with good and evil, bouts with mystery, and sense of wonder about the life beyond.

Aboard the *Sweet William* my seventeenth summer, life took on two new meanings: *texture* (the feel of the fabric of doing life in a larger systemic network) and *telos* (the fact that there is an ultimate end to existence). I discovered a crewman could walk south on decks of the oil barges being towed; yet, simultaneously, the tugboat was moving northward. While some crew members slept in bunk quarters, the *Sweet William* plowed day and night through intracoastal waters or open seas. The vessel and crew were at a new place each morning. Life moved. Life changed as part of a larger systemic process.

Imperceptibly, my explore-the-world itch learned new ways to view reality. I rediscovered through travel what I already knew: we are more than animals. As Eugene H. Peterson noted,

> There is more to being human than simply surviving; there is God . . . looking for God, pleasing God, getting God's help. We are unfinished creatures—longing, reaching, stretching towards fulfillment.

I also learned that I am not indispensable as a member of the human race. As surely as I had boarded Captain Truxillo's tugboat, the time came to leave it and capitalize on lessons gleaned from those experiences. "It's not enough to go round and round between the river and the bay," I discovered. My heart longed for the open sea. In time, I would go to officers' school in New York, become a Maritime Service officer, and a U.S. Coast Guard veteran of World War II.

Wise men and women across the centuries have sought to "tell time" not in petty disguise, but in reality. This was the experience of Viktor Frankl, an Austrian psychotherapist, who survived the Second World War concentration camp at Auschwitz. "Life in a concentration camp tore open the human soul and exposed its depths," noted Frankl.[7] The human qualities exposed in the Holocaust were a mixture of good and evil.

A more critical observation lies at the heart of his book *From Death Camp to Existentialism*. Survivors of the death camp horrors lived by a "will to meaning," akin to spiritual faith, which Frankl called an empirical fact. Persons do not live, he noted, to "satisfy a moral drive and to have a good conscience"; rather, they act "for the sake of a cause" to which they are committed, for a person whom they love, or for the sake of their God.[8] No matter how bad things got at Auschwitz, some persons survived. Their hope kept them alive.

Working with the crew of the *Sweet William* was a far cry from prisoners' experiences in German death camps. The one element they shared in common was transition—the unfinished-ness of our human story.

IT JUST KEEPS GOING AND GOING

Despite detours, life keeps on going and going—like the proverbial Energizer bunny beating a drum. Here's a woman who can handle almost anything life throws at her. But after a terrifying automobile accident, she endures a long rehabilitation therapy program and wonders, "Is this all there is?" In time, with skilled physical therapy, prescribed antidepressants, and an exercise program, she makes a comeback toward well-being.

WE THINK OF SUCH INCIDENTS AS KEY NUCLEAR EPISODES connecting the otherwise "normal" sequences of our lives. The critical event is not all of life; yet, all of life is affected by it.

When the world's first heart transplant operation was performed at Groote Schuur Hospital, in Cape Town, South Africa, December 1967, who could guess the fame thrust upon the surgeon, Christiaan N. Barnard, let alone his patient? Their lives were changed forever—to "the last heartbeat." Heart surgeries are now viewed as routine. Still, the world expects surgeons who "play God" to continue surpassing their own records. Since that is humanly impossible, their fame is usually transitory.

Making good transitions, including the best of bad situations, requires adaptive skills, a support community, genuine effort, and true resolve. Let us look at three persons' experiences in order to comprehend the life-change concept.

Making good transitions

Joey is a nine-year-old fourth grader, one of three children, whom his father described as being "unable to keep his hands off other children." When asked to clarify what he meant, the father described a selectively inattentive child whose temper outbursts led to conflicts with other children and underachieving at school.

A transition occurred when it was suggested that Joey be examined at a child study center. Diagnostic tests revealed Joey's symptoms as Attention Deficit Hyperactivity Disorder (ADD). He responded favorably to a mild prescription of Ritalin and increased parental attention. The last month of the school term, Joey's peers nominated him "most popular boy" in class. The "nuclear episode" in this instance was a careful diagnostic workup at a child study center and therapeutic steps with beneficial results.[9]

All passages are not so brief. Adolescence brings changes over nearly a decade, from about age ten in girls and twelve in boys to nearly twenty. Fran Cohen felt that crossing the boundary between childhood and adulthood would take forever. Born with a birth defect, Fran's maturation was marked by a series of surgeries. Raised in a middle-class, religious family, Fran's movement into puberty was as "normal" as possible, given the circumstances. Her physical development and sexual growth were on schedule. Intellectually, Fran was bright, but psychologically she struggled with low self-esteem. Socially, she was timid and lonely.

Aeons passed between Fran's childhood surgeries and the plastic surgery at eighteen that moved her into a new phase of social relations. Her fortitude, poise, and courage during a traditionally "stormy decade" revealed true character development. Her biological clock had said "ready," but her psychological clock had shouted "wait" on dating and traditional male-female relationships. Courtship came in due season, followed by engagement and marriage to a fine life partner. <u>Her moral values</u> <u>anchored control of her appetites and passions.</u> Patience paid off.

power to wait

> THE AGE TWENTY-SOMETHING SEARCH for meaning and power to wait are qualities needed by young adults today.

We have pictured persons facing life's transitions in childhood and youth. What of life changes in adulthood?

Jacqueline Kennedy Onassis lived a hundred lives, to paraphrase an old Chinese proverb, but only one of them really mattered—her marriage to John F. Kennedy. During her lifetime, Jackie was thrust into the role of a princess in a pillbox hat. Twice married to famous and wealthy men, she was viewed as a queen in Camelot. For many women of more common circumstances Jackie Kennedy was a vision of the ideal.

At her death in May 1994, people recalled her thousand days in the White House, beginning when she was only thirty-one. A collage of images imprinted itself deeply on the USAmerican psyche, Barbara Vobejdo reported:

> A glamorous, smiling first lady in white gloves; a stoic, grieving widow; a sexy, cosmopolitan woman who married a millionaire, then found a career in a New York publishing house.[10]

But there was a tragic side to the all-American lady who died with lymphoma in her New York apartment at the age of sixty-four. She was a private person constantly thrust into public view. A woman of high moral ideals, she lived with the fact of her first husband's reported infidelities. Preferring marriage, Jackie was twice widowed. Pushed into public life, her greatest joy was parenting John and Caroline. As a single parent and working mother, she quietly told the world that motherhood was her most important job.

Perhaps Jackie Kennedy Onassis touched women so strongly because she was both ordinary—rearing children and acting the perfect wife—and out of reach. As Vobejda said, "She was not just a fluffy princess, but a substantial strong woman."[11] Camelot was an illusion for 1960s USAmerica. The country faced racial injustices, economic uncertainties, and international problems. The Kennedy era was an illusion too good to be true. But, at the time, the world did not know it was escape from reality.

SIFTING WISDOM FROM CHANGE

Events that appear larger-than-life can traumatize the soul of an entire nation. Time staggered that November 1963 afternoon, in Dallas, Texas, when America's Camelot president, John Fitzgerald Kennedy, fell to an assassin's bullet. Time continues to magnify that fateful series of events. On the other hand, ethnologists would tell us that the constant immigration of millions of foreign-culture persons into USAmerica has changed this nation's soul more than the assassination of its first Roman Catholic president.

Mother Russia is old. Yet, the Commonwealth of Independent States (CIS) has emerged from the ashes of twentieth-century Communist Russia. Lenin's revolution of 1917–1918, that produced the Union of Soviet Socialist Republics, has dissolved into new republics. In central Asia, they possess unfamiliar names, such as Kazakhstan, Kyrgyzstan, Azerbaijan, and Uzbekistan. Georgia is not just a former Confederate stronghold in the southeastern United States. It is also an independent European republic bordering on the Black Sea.

The political and economic changes occurring in Eastern Europe may prove, in time, better for millions of inhabitants of CIS republics. Strugglers in those new nations know that walls have fallen down. They also know that keeping on with the old way of doing things no longer works.

There is a lesson for us in mapping personal and social changes. While we cannot always foresee and prepare for shifts in life's course, we can be positive in attitude, constructive in spirit, and innovative in response to life's change points.

The Hebrew and Christian scriptures, as well as secular literature, are peopled by characters touched by change—from Adam and Eve to Abraham and Sarah, from Shakespeare's King Lear to Lady Macbeth, from David and Bathsheba to the apostle Paul and Lydia of Thyatira. One thing is certain: mortals are not safe from wake-up calls.

morals are not safe from wake up calls

Attention-getters do not happen to us as the passive prisoners of history. We can make things happen—decide to attend a university, become computer literate, choose to love, commit ourselves to a marriage partner, live in a certain neighborhood, go into business, change careers, take a trip, even end life by suicide. One's attitude can make all the difference in facing life's uncertainties.

It's all in your attitude - we can make things happen

Based upon the above observations, we are more than victims shackled by alien forces. Time bears us along on the crest of changes through all of life's seasons. <u>We are in changes and changes are in us.</u> It becomes suggestive to ask, then, what are some models for finding our way?

REFLECTIVE EXERCISES

For Thought:

1. Reflect on a time of "leaving home" in your own experience. What details come to mind—painful or pleasurable happenings— about your own self-development?

2. Using the four "clocks"—biological, social, psychological, and spiritual—what time is it in each of these aspects of your life?

3. What wake-up call has touched your life the past twelve months so that all the rest of life is affected by it?

4. When you wanted to "cut and run" yet stayed the course, what person or resources helped you most?

5. What will happen if you do not work things out in some situation you are facing right now?

For Discussion:

1. How can change be better managed by having a sense of moral purpose and mission in our lives? By resistance to evil?

2. With social violence and safety needs in mind, how have public risks touched your life? Your community?

3. Given the complex matrix of personal and social transitions described here, how can we practice goodness for the world's sake?

4. What clues do kids need today for facing life's risks, relationships, and responsibilities?

5. If everything in your past is predictive of your future, how can you live more in the present and future than in the past?

NOTES

[1]Betty Clare Moffatt, *Soulwork: Clearing the Mind, Opening the Heart, Replenishing the Spirit* (Berkley CA: Wildcat Canyon Press, 1994).

[2]Erik H. Erikson, "Identity and the Life Cycle," selected papers from *Psychological Issues*, vol. 1 (New York: International Universities Press, 1959) 1, 150.

[3]Murray Bowen, M.D., "On the Differentiation of Self," *Family Therapy in Clinical Practice* (New York: Jason Aronson, 1978) 467-528.

[4]Gail Sheehy, *New Passages: Mapping Your Life Across Time* (New York: Random House, 1995) 27. Also see Richard O. Straub, *Seasons of Life Study Guide* (New York: Worth Publishers, Inc., 1990) 1-12. The guide goes with a telecourse on life-span development: *Seasons of Life*, twenty-six thirty-minute audio programs; five video programs; plus a textbook: John Kotre and Elizabeth Hall, *Seasons of Life* (Boston: Little, Brown, & Co., 1990) 23-80.

[5]Bernice L. Neugarten, a sociologist at the University of Chicago, first introduced the clock metaphors as a way of knowing what time it is through different sets of "eyes." See her "Time, Age, and the Life Cycle," *American Journal of Psychiatry*, 136 (1979) 887-93. Cf. Bernice L. Neugarten, "Interpretive Social Science and Research on Aging, " in Alice S. Rossi, ed., *Gender and the Life Course* (New York: Aldine Publishing Co., 1985) 291-300. Professor Neugarten argues that the research methods of the natural sciences are of limited value for studying life-span development in an "age-irrelevant" society.

[6]Eugene H. Peterson, *Answering God*, paper ed. (San Francisco: Harper Collins, 1991) 4.

[7]Viktor E. Frankl, *Man's Search for Meaning: An Introduction to Logotherapy*, Ilse Lasch, trans. (New York: Washington Square Press, 1963); original title: *From Death Camp to Existentialism*, 137-38.

[8]Ibid., 158.

[9]For ADHD help, see Lisa J. Bain, *A Parent's Guide to Attention Deficit Disorders* (New York: Dell Publishing, 1991).

[10]Barbara Vobejda, "Jackie Was Image of Ideal for Many," *Austin American-Statesman*, 21 May 1994, A-1, 15.

[11]Ibid.

Chapter 4

FINDING
YOUR WAY

 ACCIDENTAL WAKE-UP CALLS COME AS UNINVITED GUESTS, crashing into our private lives.

Judith Guest's novel *Ordinary People* related the crisis in seventeen-year-old Conrad Jarrett's life when he is spared in a boating accident that takes his older brother's life.[1] Her story reveals the complexity of all human relationships. With marriage and family ties already strained, the dark path of their son's untimely death deepens their difficulties.

In Guest's novel, Conrad's parents, Calvin and Beth Jarrett, are seen by outsiders as competent, successful, beautiful people. The Jarretts have it "all together." Yet, experienced internally, with Guest's genius for analyzing human nature, Beth and Calvin are deeply troubled people. Beth had played favorites and chosen Buck, the son killed on the lake, to bless. After the accident, she finds herself unable to cope when the foundations of her life were shattered. Her favorite son is dead. Husband Calvin feels helpless when the two people closest to him are hurting alone, out of his reach.

The Jarrett's teenaged, surviving son feels different in comparison with other students at his high school. He tells his psychiatrist, Dr. Berger, that he wants to get rid of his guilt feelings. They haunt his dreams and memories as an accident survivor. He wants to get rid of the past and become an ordinary teenager again.

The novel ends with the Jarretts breaking up, at least temporarily. Beth leaves Calvin and returns to her brother's home in Houston. Conrad and his father pass each other on the road that average people travel. But their navigational equipment is damaged.

"How did everything fall apart like this?" Conrad asks his father. To which the elder Jarrett replied, "It's nobody's fault. . . . It is the way things are." Ordinariness, in our lives, does not imply the absence of grief over loss, evil, and self-doubt. We are constantly being weaned from one set of attachments and surroundings and forced onto new pathways. The transition process requires us to give up prized relationships and cherished ways of doing and looking at things.

In a sense, we experience little deaths and rebirths as we move through the seasons of life. Saying goodbye to a pleasant, or an unhappy, era becomes a time of reckoning and charting a new course. Our complicity in old orders, human evil, and injustice is revealed, even as we are challenged to work for the common good.

WHAT MODELS MAY WE DEVISE for naming life's transitions and mapping our way ahead? Some observers offer only one interpretation—endings and beginnings. Others sense a spiritual dimension—experiencing God on a faith journey.

The models that follow are more than folklore. They are ways wise searchers, saints, and scholars have sought to negotiate change across time. One of the oldest and most familiar ways to picture transitions comes from the Old Testament paradigm of the Exodus.

EXODUS, WILDERNESS, AND PROMISED LAND

Persons acquainted with the Hebrew scriptures will recall Israel's 400-year sojourn in Egypt. It was trouble that brought them there in the first place. Joseph was twice sold into slavery (Gen 37–39). The patriarch Jacob's favorite son, Joseph, seemed to get everything and get away with anything. He alienated his brothers with his specialness and wild dreams. He was the "blessed" one (1 Chron 5:2; Gen 35:22). Jacob's twelve sons were from four different mothers—wives Leah and Rachel, and concubines Bilhah and Zilpah. The boys were half-brothers in what became a dysfunctional family system. Eventually, even the blessed child had his dreams dashed.

One of the hardest things to lose in life is a dream. We desire a career, a mate, an education, a fantasy vacation, an ideal house, the privilege of parenting, freedom of choice, good health, a true friendship. We learn from the life of Joseph how to survive broken dreams. Instead of an exhalted position over his jealous brothers, Joseph was forced into slavery in Egypt. His brothers thought him dead.

Even a short version of historic events in that mid-Eastern world is complex. The Israelites turned to Egypt for foodstuffs in a great famine. Jacob's sons crossed the desert to Joseph's land in order to gain grain. To their embarrassment and horror, their "dead" brother, Joseph, was the equivalent of Egypt's prime minister under the ruling pharaoh. They got better than they bargained for—grain and more—a glad reunion with the brother they assumed was dead.

Joseph had been abused—betrayed, rejected, cut-off from family. Now, he offers his offenders community. He repairs relationships by offering them familyness, the very thing they had denied him. With God's help, Joseph gave up any desire to judge and punish his brothers. To offer forgiveness to an offender does not guarantee the transaction. There must be reciprocity. But Joseph offered even more—sanctuary in a distant land. All too soon, the gift turned sour. Jacob's descendants became the Egyptians' slave.

Four hundred years passed—almost twice the span US-America has been a republic. The book of Exodus records the birth of Moses, a redeemer figure in Israelite history. Reared as the son of royalty, Moses was forty when his sympathies for his abused, people provoked him to murder an Egyptian (Exod 2:11-25). Fleeing to the remote wilderness of Midian, he shepherded his father-in-law Jethro's flocks another forty years. Married and the father of two sons, Moses had settled into nomadic life.

You may recall the sequence of events: bush aglow, voice of God, vision of liberation, self-doubt of his ability and leader skills; yet, divine assignment to lead the Israelites from Egypt into the promised land (Exod 3-5). Following forty years of wilderness wandering and prediction that their leader would not enter the promised land, Israel crossed over Jordan under Joshua's leadership (Josh 1-3). A radical, new beginning of claiming Cannan—the country God promised to Abraham, Isaac, and Jacob—had begun.

There is wisdom to be found in various studies of catch-22 situations that may block us from success or move us beyond some double bind.[2] While the transformations experienced in our fast-paced lives may be viewed merely as natural phenomena, Exodus sees divine factors at work as well. It is the inner and underlying process common to all transitions that keys in to the threefold dynamic of letting go, in-betweenness, and new beginnings.

ENDINGS, THE NEUTRAL ZONE, BEGINNINGS

Most observers of our changing world comment about endings, the neutral zone, and new beginnings in life's passages. West Coast commentator, William Bridges has followed this threefold transition process model in his consultations with social nomads, middle-aged executives, and CEOs of major corporations.[3] Bridges generalized from his personal experience in the 1960s when he moved his family from an academic setting to a remote habitat, away from modern life's pressures. Bridges is also familiar with works by self theorists, such as Erik Erikson; human development specialists, such as Daniel Levinson and Roger Gould; and investigative reporters, such as Gail Sheehy.[4] He weaves their more technical findings into his classical humanities background.

As a literary specialist, Bridges owes a great debt to Greek mythology, particularly the heroism of Odysseus in *The Odyssey*. His philosophical cues range from Lao Tzu's *Tao Te Ching* to Mircea Eliade's *The Sacred and the Profane*. But it was the Dutch anthropologist Arnold van Gennep who opened for Bridges a threefold path of adult development: separation, transition, and incorporation.[5] A student of traditional societies who took pains to mark stages along life's way, van Gennep coined the term rites of passage for Westerners.

 THE INNER WORK OF ADAPTATION INVOLVES STRUGGLE though one's outer situation appears serene.

Take, for example, the case of a CEO who "lost the war" in a struggle for company control and was forced to resign. He was given a brief period of time to vacate his office. A gifted person may move physical furnishings, personal belongings, files, wall hangings, and the "other stuff" but fail to come to terms with loss and separation. Following such events, the inner work of grief management and adaptation goes on. A person facing ouster and new beginnings needs community support and courage for oneself to make things easier.

"Not everything vanishes in the ending process," noted Bridges, and "some people find it very important to experience the continuities in their lives when so much else is changing."[6] He illustrated by referring to a table his parents purchased before he was born, from which meals were served in his childhood, a table that symbolized his New England roots and upbringing. Using the table as a work station for writing in California tethered him to his background. With much changing in his life, Bridges took comfort in things that remained in place. Some of life's most dramatic changes come, not from losses, betrayals, or disappointments, but from fresh vision.

VISION, JOURNEY, AND RETURN

Still another model for facing life's transitions is to appreciate transactions that spring from quiet reflection and redefinition, fresh resolve, times of spiritual searching, revisioning values, nurturing dreams, and obeying the Inner Voice. It is not a coincidence that individuals recovering from near-death experiences feel "spared for a purpose." There is new sensitivity and appreciation of time, work, nature, and relationships. The mundane is shadowed in mystery. Life blooms with fresh resolve to make a difference in the world.

Biblical characters—such as Abraham and Sarah, Moses, Samuel and his mother Hannah, Mary the mother of Jesus, and Saul of Tarsus—changed life courses as the result of experiencing a sense of the holy, a burning bush, a voice in the night calling one by name, an angelic presence, or a blinding light. Israel's King David was provoked to repentance by the simple parable of a greedy rich man, told by Nathan the prophet. Isaiah saw the Lord "high and lifted up" in a temple epiphany after King Uzziah's death. He was to work as God's spokesperson, warning Israel of impending disaster; yet, reminding them God would do "a new thing" in the nation's history (Isa 43:19).

Though far removed in time, the remarkable vision experienced by Constantine the Great in 312 A.D. changed the course of Western history. Reportedly, during a battle at the Milvian Bridge in Rome, Constantine is said to have seen the sign of the cross in the noonday sky. Words in Greek, "By this sign conquer!" (usually given in Latin, *in hoc signo vinces*) prompted him to turn the Roman Empire toward God and the holy Catholic church. Under moral conviction as he established a new capital in Byzantium, named Constantinople, the emperor abolished the system of branding the faces of convicts, punished masters who killed their slaves, and published an edict of toleration insuring freedom of conscience throughout the Empire.

The crusades of the Middle Ages were bold expeditions during which persons of high idealism set out to free the Holy Land from Islamic control, liberate persons from religious or political dominance, and bring honor to some king or queen.

LIFE DOES NOT ALWAYS GIVE US GRAND CRUSADES, but it does give us chances.

It was the visionary president John F. Kennedy who inspired a nation to put persons on the moon. Admiral Alan Shepard, first American astronaut in space and famed moon golfer, told the "inside story of America's race to the moon" on the twenty-fifth anniversary of the first moon landing.[7] That was 1969. What will global and planetary exploration be like in 2009?

Half a century ago, Anne Frank—symbol of the 1,500,000 Jewish children who died during the Holocaust—wrote a fairytale about an imaginary bear with a vision. "Blurry" was a naughty runaway bear who wanted to "discover the world." Today, Blurry is a metaphor for trapped persons all over the world who wish to escape, travel, and return with heroic tales. The story is a heartcry from a young woman whose world for twenty-five months was limited to a window looking out upon a chestnut tree, a small street, a canal, and some neighboring houses in Amsterdam.

When the young bear returns home to his mother, Anne wrote:

> "Blurry, why did you run away?" "I wanted to discover the world," Blurry answered. "And did you discover it?" "Oh, I saw a lot, a great deal, and now I am a very clever bear. . . . But I could not find the world!"[8]

While Anne Frank was not permitted to survive the killing instincts of the German occupiers of Holland, at fifteen she understood much about humankind. She and her sister, Margot, died of malnutrition and typhus in the Bergen-Belsen death camp in Germany in March 1945, two months before World War II ended in Europe. Remarkably, it is Anne's diary, translated into more than fifty languages, that provides her "forever young" immortality. Her spiritual vision and physical travels limited by events of war, Anne survives in our hearts as a major character on history's stage.

More than three decades ago, a young Texas woman named Rebekah Naylor dreamed of going to India as a Christian missionary surgeon. After graduating from Vanderbilt University School of Medicine, she completed a surgical residency at Parkland Hospital in Dallas. A large public hospital linked with the University of Texas Southwestern Medical School, Parkland was a good place to prepare for life in Bangalore, India. Human needs there never stopped. In 1974, Dr. Naylor arrived at her new post, half a world away from her parents and childhood home in USAmerica.

The story of Naylor's impact on thousands of patients' lives in Bangalore Baptist Hospital is fascinating. She has inspired high standards of professional service among the national medical staff. Working in south India, in an area where 45,000,000 people live, she has touched many lives for God. In one recent year, the 143-bed hospital staff treated more than 7,000 inpatients; performed 1,800 operations; and some 1,200 babies were delivered.

Because of the legal climate regarding expatriates, the physician has had to fight the system in order to practice medicine in a land of unending needs. Her inspiring vision includes not only performing life-giving surgeries, but also founding a new school of nursing, and sharing the true light of Christianity in a world of varied religious viewpoints.

LOSS, GRIEF, AND RECOVERY

Thus far, we have examined three models for mapping change and navigating life's transitions: (1) separations sparked by exodus (leavings), wilderness, and promised land; (2) endings, neutral zone, and beginnings; and (3) vision, journey, and return. Phoenix-like stories with generally positive outcomes have accompanied each model. We understand matters could go the other way. Some events, for instance, death, are final. Some conflicted relationships and mean-spirited individuals appear intransigent. Cut-offs do come in families for which no remedy appears. Nations in the Middle East seem constantly poised for battle.

Loss and grief have a way of narrowing life's landscape. Unwanted changes come upon us: for example, a drive-by homicide in a drug-dealing neighborhood, a fateful industrial accident, or death of a loved one during heart bypass surgery. Long-term hopes for the family of a brilliant teenager shut down when he or she commits suicide. No cars, no clothes, no college, no comradeship, nobody to care for is there. Only memories remain.

Losses in life bring changes—whether the slow, uneven deterioration of one's health or marriage or a quick loss such as a residential fire. A couple moved into their son's house following an electrical fire that completely destroyed their residence. Memorabilia, art, jewelry, porcelains from the Far East, furniture, linens, clothing, medical and financial records, books, family photographs, and cookware—everything was lost. Working with their insurance adjuster brought added distress. Their house and possessions were underinsured, according to "fine print" in their homeowner's policy. Their indemnity fell far short of the cost of reconstructing their residence on the original foundation site. Fortunately, they are people of strong faith who believe that "life is more [important] than food" and "the body more [important] than clothing" (Matt 6:25). Still, their losses have been hard to accept.

Downsizing happens. Competition from global conglomerates and low-budget competitors forces business giants to slim down. Job shakeups come. To love and to work, Sigmund Freud once told his disciple, Erik Erikson, are twin essentials of mature living. Without work, a person becomes a member of an endangered species.

What does a fifty-four-year-old executive who is pink-slipped do? Some individuals change careers, others retool, some retire, others become consultants. Still others pay exorbitant fees to corporate headhunters who guarantee new employment within 90 to 120 days. Some ex-employees develop physical symptoms; others give up and prematurely die. California therapist Marsha Sinetar advises persons forced to revise their careers: "Do what you love; the money will follow."[9]

Tom Moore reflected on the prospect of his retirement: "I am beginning to feel redundant around here. Some of the younger guys are pushing me to retire and get out of the way." With two earned doctoral degrees and more than four decades in a career track, his talents are valuable. Now, Moore is experiencing anticipatory grief in giving up his career. His journey will not be recovery but *discovery* of a new pathway in post-retirement years.

There is a lesson here for baby boomers, eager to take over businesses, institutions, wealth, power, and politics from their parents' generation. Emily Dickinson wrote in *The Belle of Amhurst*: "Hold your parents tenderly, for the world will seem a strange and distant place when they are gone." Our growing numbers of sage citizens need to feel they are more than useless "knots on a log." Persons in the senior years can become our models and mentors—true pioneers of the future.

Transition management through loss, bereavement, and recovery wears many masks. Each person grieves in his or her own way. Death is final, but its management and aftermath varies culture by culture over the world. While a few aboriginal tribes may place ailing elders in desolate areas for wild animals to devour, other cultures follow prescribed rituals and bury valuable possessions with the deceased tribe member. Until recent years, surviving members of the Chilimacha Indian nation, in south Louisiana, hung a dead person's corpse in a tree for a prescribed period. Not only body fluids drained, but one's spirit took final flight before interment.

In many parts of the world, the family prepares a corpse for burial. It may place the earthly remains in the ground or on a funeral pyre. Following death in Western nations, "banking" organs for transplant purposes is not uncommon. As to funeral rites, cremation is preferred by some families; whereas, elaborate memorial services are preferred by others. A religious funeral service may provide consolation and community support to grieving survivors precisely because it opens one to an eternal, hopeful perspective.

Socially sanctioned support groups have become part of what holds our society together in times of profound change. This leads us to consider how life is sustained in times of traumatic stress.

TRAUMA, POST-TRAUMATIC STRESS, AND ADAPTATION

The feedback loop of response to traumatic events is closely akin to the loss, grief, recovery model above. In trauma the degree of change intensifies. The horror of a situation may be heightened. The magnitude of some loss may be almost incomprehensible. The terrorist bombing of Pan Am Flight 103 over Lockerbie, Scotland, during the 1988 Christmas season shocked the world. It was not just the fiery deaths of 270 people, unknown personally to most of us. The trauma lay in how it happened, when it happened, in its senseless tragedy, and the seeming powerlessness of all parties to have prevented it.[10]

Whether it is a father's rape of his preteen daughter that shames her into lost innocence, toxic emotion, and mistrust of men, or a spouse's accidental death on the job—traumas happen. We describe the impact with phrases such as "hard hit, unreal, tough, unbelievable, horrible, unforgettable, depressing." Neighbors are traumatized when an entire family perishes in a house fire where windows were barred and doors were bolted for security. Feelings of helplessness pervade mass death in an inferno in events such as the 1996 ValueJet crash in Florida's Everglades or the tragic TWA 800 explosion off the Long Island, New York, coast that claimed 230 persons' lives in the same year.

Persons responding to traumatic events tend to get caught up in the shocking drama. One relives an automobile accident, for example, in which a child is crushed or a passenger is brain-damaged for life. Witnesses to Rwanda's dreadful tribal massacres, in which countless lives were destroyed, continue to experience toxic emotions and somatic symptoms. Trauma team members working where Delta 191 crashed—in 1985, killing 137 people—were themselves severely shaken by such horror.

An incident reported about the noted nineteenth-century pulpiteer, Charles Haddon Spurgeon, illustrates the struggle of adaptation. The fame of the twenty-two-year-old preacher, in London, had prompted him to rent Surrey Music Hall for worship. On one occasion, in October 1856, the vast auditorium with its three galleries was filled with an audience of 10,000 persons. Just as Spurgeon stood to speak, someone shouted, "Fire! Fire! The galleries are giving way. The place is falling!" In the mad scramble toward exits that followed, seven people were crushed to death. Many others were seriously injured.

Gradually, it became apparent there was no fire. A voice of illness or evil, or both, from an undetected attendee had prompted the stampede. Though order was finally restored, the shaken young orator collapsed after learning seven persons had died and nearly thirty had been taken to the hospital. For two weeks he recalled the tragic events, lost sleep, wept, and experienced nightmares. One day, while walking in a quiet garden at the home of a friend, a Scripture verse came to mind: "Therefore God also highly exalted him [Jesus Christ] and gave him the name that is above every name" (Phil 2:9). It is reported that Spurgeon determined, thereafter, to magnify his Master's name—not his own reputation.

He returned to the great music hall and for three years, 1856–1859, proclaimed God's message to eager hearers. Post-traumatic stress was a reality in Spurgeon's life. Authors Beeson and Hunsicker report, he "was plagued the rest of his ministry by depression, discouragement, illness, and fatigue."[11] His profound faith in God helped Spurgeon to endure and minister to others over a span of three decades.

Therapists who seek to assist persons devastated by tragic events tend to follow an orderly process of trauma treatment. Because hurting persons are aided through identifying with and hearing the stories of other wounded persons, caregivers usually provide group therapy. They are sensitive to numerous factors that may influence a person's recovery rate, for instance:

- one's childhood (previous) experiences with traumatic events
- availability of ongoing care from a person's support community
- one's religious faith, attitudes, or values that may sustain
- the potential for reoccurrence of the hurtful circumstance or event (For example, will a survivor of parental rape become a continuous victim? Will she or he face threats and more sex abuse?)
- violation of person's values or deep losses that were experienced during trauma-causing events
- the individual's degree of emotional health or pathology
- identity and relationship issues that must be resolved

 LOOK FOR THE TEACHABLE MOMENT in trauma resolution therapy.

Trauma resolution therapy through group process usually begins with introductions and debriefing. A covenant of confidentiality is established, and ground rules are laid for what must be kept in the group and what may be shared outside. It is generally acceptable to comment on group process, but not content or personal details.

In therapy sessions, group members are free to identify any issues that may have wounded them or hurt others. They are free to detail facts about the incident(s). More important than any datapoint is the person's deepest feelings, reactions, and symptoms transpiring since the event(s).

Transition management goes beyond experience and toxic feelings, however unusual, to assimilation and life planning. A wise therapist educates her or his clients with a plan of action. Reassurance cannot be shallow. Future risks, painful situations, even unrelated incidents should be anticipated. Therapeutic closure comes when the recovering person acknowledges readiness to move on with life. Friendships formed during the group process may continue beyond the trauma resolution therapy.

The potential for maladaptive and pathological responses lies close at hand, whatever therapeutic model one follows. There may be no "promised land" in view, only the despair and hopelessness of flashbacks, low pay-offs, and defeats.

To summarize, finding your way may not fit any of these five models. You may have a marvelous dream of how things ought to be—a model marriage, an ideal living arrangement, a healthy child, or satisfaction at work. On the other hand, you may doubt your ability to achieve a goal and may deny yourself the satisfaction of accomplishing an objective. Facing changes and uncertainties is a tonic for some individuals. They get "turned on" by challenges. Less secure persons, having been wounded along life's way, behave (unconsciously) so that they continue to feel hurt or face rejection.

As much as anything else, we desire to learn from people who have managed life-changes well. Discovering pathways to change management will claim our attention next. Meanwhile, check out the following ideas for thought and discussion.

REFLECTIVE EXERCISES

For Thought:

1. Imagine yourself moving from your present residence and work assignment to a new locale, for example, from the San Francisco area to Colorado Springs. What model discussed here for facing transitions would best fit your circumstances?

2. Recall a life dream in which you deeply wished to make a key change: in education, work, marriage, family, or living arrangement. Where are you in the change management process with your dream(s)?

3. Reread some of the stories from life in chapter 4. Are there parallels with your own experience? Note how you connect with some of the "others."

4. How can adaptive skills be nurtured and strengthened at home, in church or synagogue, or in the "public square?"

For Discussion:

1. Ask members of your group to review the transition models supplied in chapter 4. Of the five models, which pathway describes your lifemapping process best?

2. Suppose a good friend discusses privately with you the fact that her brother, now living in New York, has AIDS. Their family has not revealed the tragedy at church or to friends. She wants to know how to break out of the box of silence. What would you suggest? What if he were your own brother?

3. Is it possible at age twenty-two, like Charles Spurgeon, the noted nineteenth-century pulpiteer, to feel oneself a failure in life? Who is there for you when you face tragedy, shame, or sorrow?

4. What forces in our social environment have the potential to divide families, across generations, for example, sexual orientation, abortion, or organ donation?

5. When transitions come, what are the primary resources that see you through? How may you, in turn, offer support to other mapmakers?

NOTES

[1]Judith Guest, *Ordinary People* (New York: Viking Press, 1976).

[2]Russell Chandler, *Racing Toward 2001: The Forces Shaping America's Religious Future* (San Francisco: Harper San Francisco, 1992); Francis Dorff, *The Art of Passingover* (Mahwah NJ: Paulist Press, 1988); Kathleen Hall Jamieson, *Beyond the Double Bind: Women and Leadership* (New York: Oxford University Press, 1995); J. Bill Ratliff, *When You Are Facing Change* (Louisville KY: Westminster/John Knox Press, 1989); and Stephen Strasser and John Sena, *Transitions: Successful Strategies from Mid-Career to Retirement* (Hawthorne NJ: Career Press, 1990).

[3]William Bridges, *Transitions: Making Sense of Life's Changes* (Reading MA: Addison-Wesley, 1980) 89-150.

[4]Erik H. Erikson, *Identity, Youth, and Crisis* (New York: W. W. Norton, 1968); Roger Gould, *Transformations: Growth and Change in the Adult Years* (New York: Simon and Schuster, 1978); Daniel J. Levinson, *The Seasons of a Man's Life* (New York: Alfred Knopf, 1978); and Gail Sheehy, *New Passages: Mapping Your Life Across Time* (New York: Random House, 1995).

[5]See Arnold van Gennep, *Rites of Passage*, trans. Monika B. Vizedom and Gabrielle L. Chaffee (Chicago: University of Chicago Press, 1960).

[6]Bridges, 148-49.

[7]Alan Shepard, *Moon Shot: The Inside Story of America's Race to the Moon* (Atlanta: Turner Publishing, 1994).

[8]Anne Frank, quoted in A. James Rudin, "Forever in Our Hearts," *Fort Worth Star-Telegram*, 5 June 1994, C8.

[9]Marsha Sinetar, *Do What You Love: The Money Will Follow* (Mahwah NJ: Paulist Press, 1986).

[10]A Palestinian follower of terrorist mastermind Abu Nidal told a Beirut court, 13 June 1994, that he carried out the 1988 bombing of Pan Am Flight 103 over Lockerbie, Scotland; but his confession was termed a hoax.

[11]Ray Beeson and Ranelda Mack Hunsicker, *The Hidden Price of Greatness* (Wheaton IL: Tyndale House, 1991) 52.

Chapter 5

PATHWAYS TO
CHANGE MANAGEMENT

The name Christopher Reeve is well known in American folklore because of his *Superman* television stardom. The forty-three-year-old actor, now married to Dana Morosini, age thirty-two, was paralyzed from the shoulders down in a horse riding accident, May 28, 1995. Reeve has been a risker and sports enthusiast who enjoyed flying, sailing, scuba diving, ice hockey, soccer and, with tragic consequences, competitive horse riding.

In a television interview four months after his injury, Reeve said, "When I do a sport, I take it to as high a level as I can go."[1] Even then, he was seated in a wheelchair that he activated by blowing into a straw. The riding accident in Virginia broke his neck and landed Reeve at the Kessler Institute in West Orange, New Jersey, for rehabilitation. He's convinced he will walk again, but has no idea how or when. He admitted to fleeting suicidal thoughts, but claimed a mind-over-matter edge: "Your body is not you," he said. "Your mind and spirit take over." Reeve credits his family's love and fidelity for the strength to go on living.

The actor made no claim to religious persuasion during that or a subsequent interview. But he affirmed the healing power of hope. "There's something else coming. I don't know what it is, but I've got to find it." He reported having received more than 100,000 letters from supportive fans. Improving with therapy, Reeve plans to direct TV programming and invest in other peoples' lives.

 HELPLESSNESS IS A COMMON FEELING when life spins out of control, injuries happen, or when things don't go as we had planned.

A shift does not have to be negative for one to experience struggle. Things may look favorable. Here is a winner of millions of dollars in a lottery whose distant relatives descend like vultures on prey. Such a "lucky person" is often bombarded by salespersons and promoters of financial scams. What appears to have been a good thing forces a lottery winner into a self-protective, defensive posture. Many persons do not survive success! A marriage made with good intentions, but not in good faith, may be doomed from the start. Even an Olympic champion may battle cancer and die.

Is there any wisdom to help a person "take a hit" or survive an upturn in life, then bounce back? Other mapmakers' discoveries may help you chart your journey.

REDISCOVER MYTH AND FANTASY

A character from Greek mythology—Proteus, the gifted wise man of the sea—furnishes a metaphor of sustainability and the capacity for reconstructing a life strategy. Proteus was a survivor, sought after for his wisdom and admired for his ability of self-transformation. What can we denizens of modern culture learn from this ancient myth?

Endowed with the gift of prophecy, Proteus knew *all* things— past, present, and future—but hesitated telling what he knew.[2] Those who wished to consult the sage had first to surprise and bind him while he slept. Even when caught, Proteus would try to escape by employing all sorts of shapes. He could assume any form—animal or plant, fire or water—to avoid his enemies. Because of his powers of adaptability and survivorship, Proteus was regarded by some as a symbol of original matter. He modeled rebirth in the seasons of life.

One of Proteus' most interesting characteristics was his capacity for self-transformation. His gift to us is innovation— creative adaptability in difficult circumstances. Furthermore, Proteus resided in the ocean depths—an ancient symbol of danger, darkness, destructive currents, and the dwelling place of monster leviathans of the sea. His legacy reminds us that life is spent in mystery and grace. It's possible there isn't a quick or easy solution to life's conundrums. After all, much of living is a complex riddle with no easy answers.

African myths and legends, retold by Kathleen Arnott, are rich with change themes. She and her husband recorded tribal tales in many African nations, and then translated them into English. Stories of African peoples illustrate their fierce sense of justice, powers of patience and endurance, and mastery as storytellers.[3] She relates myths of magic drums, flying horses, evil witches, mysterious pumpkins, and of a greedy spider. Storytellers explain why flies buzz, why the sun and moon live in the sky, why the crab has no head, and why the bat flies at night. Such tales invite us to mirthful imagination and to innovate solutions to life's challenges.

 GROWNUPS ARE VICTIMIZED by unused play and unlived fantasy.

Three professional men were reminded of their lost fantasy worlds during lunch one day at a neighborhood restaurant. A young mother, her ten-year-old daughter, and a friend were seated next to the male luncheoners. Surprisingly, the girl had a bear-friend in tow, almost as large as herself, whom she sat in the chair next to her. His role in her rich imaginative life soon was obvious. She kept propping bear-boy up properly and attending to his needs as she munched on animal cookies.

"Did he order a meal?" one of the men inquired, as the three-some got up to leave. "No," she shyly replied.

"She was going to give him some animal cookies," said her mother, "until she realized she might end up asking him to eat a bear. He's skipping lunch." While three females were at the table, a fourth "person" was quite present—the boy-bearfriend.

Jesuit psychologist Anthony de Mello reminds us that fantasy is a way to God, "an untapped source of power" in life. Serious-minded, anxiety-prone USAmericans have turned fantasy and magic over to CD-ROM and "comic" books. What children enjoy at theme parks many adults endure. Such a pilgrimage appears sheer escape from reality. Yet, Anthony de Mello holds that true fantasy helps us "plunge more deeply into present reality—to perceive it better and to come to grips with it with renewed vigor."[4] Who could have dreamed in the summer of 1969 that earthlings would visit the moon, a quarter million miles out in space? Play golf on the moon, collect moon rocks, write one's initials in moon dust—impossible! Yet, the Buck Rogers magic of early science fiction became reality. Many adults actually enjoy mall walking, outlet mall trips, and escaping to theme parks.

Adaptation to change may require us to give up our atrophied powers of fantasy and jaded imaginations. Creativeness, the novelty of exploring various scenarios as options, often leads one "out of the woods" and into the clearing. An "ah-ha" moment comes when, like a butterfly drying its wings after cocoon birth, renewal happens. While children are apprentices to the adult world, they have much to teach us about pleasure, the power to fantasize, and playful ways to endure life's shifting fortunes.

While a rich fantasy life may open us to innovative change management, one's faith in God is the true ground of realistic hope.

REMEMBER THE FAITHKEEPERS

The Hebrew Scriptures reveal the legacy of God's care for people in perilous circumstances. During one of ancient Israel's toughest eras—a nation exiled far from home—God promised: "I know the plans I have for you, . . . to give you a future with hope" (Jer 29:11). The prophet Jeremiah's hearers faced life-threatening circumstances, yet, they were called on to endure.

 OUR RELIGIOUS REMEMBRANCE, a healthy obsession with God, can help us endure the confusion of profound displacement.

In early Hebrew history, it was noted that the patriarch Abraham looked "forward to the city that has foundations, whose architect and builder is God" (Heb 11:10). He and Sarah were promised a child in their old age to carry on the family line and to provide a world blessing. Isaac's birth became a reality in late life. Persons in the biblical world saw God as the Lord of history, able to intervene in human situations with changes beyond their boldest imagination. It is in that confidence that today's change-survivor puts old ways aside and faces new challenges.

It was said that Moses "persevered as though he saw him who is invisible" (Heb 11:27). That description came more than 1,500 years after Moses' death. He was a towering figure of faith and wise leader of a new nation.

In a similar vein, Joshua, who had succeeded Moses and lived to old age, called Israel's elders together for a farewell. He reminded them of God's fidelity as a covenant-keeper. "You know in your hearts and souls . . . that not one thing has failed of all the good things that the Lord your God promised concerning you"

(Josh 23:14b). Students of Hebrew history enjoy the story of Queen Esther who interceded with the Persian King Xerxes for her people. Mordecai had encouraged her thus: "Who knows? Perhaps you have come to royal dignity for just such a time as this" (Esther 4:14b). She became a nation's compelling first lady and spiritual leader.

 LESSONS FROM ANCIENT PATHFINDERS GUIDE US like bright stars that transcend circumstances and cultural contexts. They encourage us to move beyond shallow self-indulgence to deep springs from which great rivers of life flow.

What do these faithkeepers have in common to guide us? They were down-to-earth followers of one who had "plans" for their future. Psychoanalyst Carl Jung typed persons thus: (1) *Thinking types* are motivated by an idea. (2) *Intuitive types* may be guided by a vision. (3) *Sensate types* need a plan. (4) *Feeling types* need everyone around them to share in an undertaking. People experience similar events uniquely, according to their temperament. We need a divine compass to guide us through life's complexity.

Tennyson's *Ulysses* said it well:

I am a part of all that I have met;
Yet all experience is an arch wherethro'
Gleams that untravell'd world, whose margin fades
For ever and for ever when I move.

We can imagine the nineteenth-century English poet in Italy, viewing a great Roman arch, constructed more than a thousand years before. Like one's own shadow, life is an arched horizon that moves with us as we move. The open road is a metaphor for continual pilgrimage, however rough the terrain or fierce the inhabitants along the way.

We who live in the interactive, electronic world of cellular telephones, telecomputers, fiber optics e-mail, and television must slow down long enough to learn to read again. Gifted writers bear concern for their readers. Despite scanners and electronic libraries promised for the future, a rich literary legacy is within our reach.

LEARN TO READ AGAIN

Writers with active imaginations can transport us to many destinations. Jimmy is a thirteen-year-old who dreams of traveling to the frozen land of Antarctica. Some adult friends, upon learning about his travel fantasy, presented him with an eye-catching, color pictorial book featuring that mystical continent. Antarctica beckons as part of Jimmy's future story.

Novelists can transport us from love scenes set mid the bridges of Madison County, Iowa, to dazzling cities of Europe, filled with intrigue, violence, and danger. Plots can be mystery thrillers or boring monstrosities. In our reading tastes, like art, beauty resides in the eye of the beholder. Who, for example, needs *Chicken Soup for the Soul* let alone a "second and third helping?" Apparently a huge reader market, hungry for inspirational food in bite-sized servings.

Several contemporary writers have spoken to me from the vantage point of their own inquiries.[5] Investigative reporter and political journalist Gail Sheehy is well known for her landmark work *Passages*, as well as for her frankness about menopause, *The Silent Passage*. But it is her fascinating proposal of a second adulthood, for persons ages forty-five to eighty-five, in *New Passages: Mapping Your Life Across Time* that intrigues me. Sheehy's yearning for meaning in midlife (she is now in her fifties) spurred her creative effort.

Sheehy's book is the product of extensive research surveys among professionals and working-class USAmericans. She showcases findings that compare five generations, extracted from fifty years of U.S. Census reports. The author blends a social scientist's ability to synthesize data with a novelist's gift for story-telling. Her creative map of adult life proposes a *second adulthood*, extending well into what she terms the "uninhibited eighties." Sheehy helps us make sense of our own transitions by identifying with other people like ourselves.

Jimmy Allen and I are contemporaries. He and I were fellow classmates under the tutelage of the late Christian ethicist Thomas Buford Maston. Since our theological training we have followed separate paths, both of us in religious occupations. His *Burden of a Secret: A Story of Truth and Mercy in the Face of AIDS* takes interested readers through the valley of the shadow of death.

Allen's story discloses his shock, dismay, and confusion upon learning in 1985 that his daughter-in-law, Lydia, and grandsons, Bryan and Matthew, had tested positive for the HIV virus. A California blood bank notified his son, Scott, that the blood Lydia received when Matthew was born was contaminated with the AIDS virus. Grief piled onto grief when the Colorado congregation where Scott served asked him to resign when he told leaders about his family's illness.

Lydia and Bryan died quickly from their fatal infections. Matt lingered in hospice care through his thirteenth birthday. He has since died. Skip, one of Allen's three sons has AIDS. Their eldest son, Mike, has been diagnosed as a schizophrenic; though, with treatment, he leads a useful life. His wife, Wanda, has "known the agonies of depression" with bipolar personality.[6]

No longer able to hide the burden of his family's secret, Allen's book is a clear call to congregations and synagogues to deal compassionately with AIDS patients and their families. He says his son, Scott, likely suffered most because of the church's rejection of his AIDS-diseased family. The author claims God is greater than organized religion—an insight discovered since son Scott has turned to Eastern religions for spiritual direction.

The Allen family's biological, emotional, and social clocks have been shattered. But the clan's father is a sojourner of profound faith. His volume is both a lament and a call for action. Allen challenges us to abandon what he calls our "leave-it-to-the-Samaritan- complex" and asks congregations to demonstrate real compassion. Allen's map of the treacherous ravages of AIDS shows the way for other persons who face the dark.

 THERE ARE POETS AND POLITICIANS, philosophers and artists, photo/video journalists and lyricists, and comedians and composers—all storytellers.

One of the most published map makers of our time is William Bennett. His massive tomes, *The Book of Virtues* and *The Moral Compass*, are heavy with moralistic stories.[7] Famous names from the past and present of literature reveal their values and call leaders to serious reflection.

In the author's preface, at the outset, I said that you and I live in the postmodern world where life is being redefined. The term *postmodern* has varied meanings. None among us has a better grasp on the impact of postmodernism in the West, in my judgment, than James W. Fowler. His *Faithful Change: The Personal and Public Challenges of Postmodern Life* blends theoretical assumptions about faith development, shame's effects on conscience and culture, and the practical outworkings of postmodernism for theological understanding, family responsibilities, and social ethics.

My own understanding of postmodern paradigm shifts reflects indebtedness to Fowler, though we function with distinct convictions and conclusions. Three things are clear from his discussion, which I am casting in a more popular style. One, postmodernists hold that basic assumptions of the eighteenth-century Enlightenment, grounded in universal reason and the inevitability of human progress, no longer serve the world's pluralistic societies well. Two, given our advanced technological systems for networking, with a worldwide web for instantaneous communication, people live with new forms of consciousness. New paradigms for facing reality and shaping truth knit the globe's inhabitants into new cultures.

Modernity is also giving way in the realm of faith and religious expression. We see movements away from appeals to universal reason, favoring the interests of society's ruling classes, to an appreciation for more traditional religious expressions. Common-sense wisdom in worship practices and ethical grounding in the social order are further evidences of postmodernism.

What one reads, like what one eats, depends upon one's appetite, health, IQ, schedule, mood, and intent. What serves as escape for one reader may provide information for another. People read from the silly to the significant—often gulping down a literary diet too fast to digest its substance. Some of us read as work; some as play; some as entertainment. Whatever one's purpose, wise writers may help us face expectantly life's toughest transitions.

One way literary and artistic figures affect culture is opening people to the unexpected. Artists catch the flow of historic change first, followed by philosophers with wise platitudes, and politicians who pass new laws and create new structures. Unfortunately, it is often the church and religious guides that come last to the work of transition. This leads us to observe that would-be seers of change must be open to the unexpected.

BE OPEN TO THE UNEXPECTED

He was rushing along a major department store corridor when our eyes met. Quickly, the tall, well-dressed, and balding man revealed momentary recognition and then resumed his pace. I spoke first; then he stopped. There were mutual reintroductions and handshakes after a two-decade interlude. Andy Johnson is a graduate of Harvard Medical School and a top surgeon.

"You helped save my wife's life in 1975," I reminded him. "Thyroid surgery. Do you remember?"

"Oh, yes," the physician responded, "I knew we had met somewhere . . . just couldn't recall where or when. How is your wife?"

"Fine. She takes a thyroid substitute each day. We both remain in your debt for a good surgical procedure. By the way, how is your practice going?"

"I just closed my office two days ago," came the rejoinder.

"Hum-m-m; so, you are retiring. What will you be doing to make good use of your time?" His smile reassured me: "I'll be teaching part-time at University Hospital." He seemed relieved to say he was headed from something (an ending) into some new endeavor (a neutral zone), but was indefinite about duration of the arrangement.

USAmericans have endowed physicians with divinity. Perhaps we commoners have made them kings and queens of the health kingdom. Together, we have helped them say, "Come, let us play God." But when they fail to insure life and vitality, or make an honest mistake, or an error in judgment that threatens a patient's life, watch out. The M.D. who earns $150,000 a year, less or more according to specialty, can be subjected to a malpractice suit for minor cause.

Our reverence for life and for physicians who help sustain it makes the following confession even more surprising. The unexpected conversation, related by a wise minister, contains lessons for us all.[8]

"When I finished medical school, I thought I had learned a lot," the young cardiologist said. "We studied hard, digested a huge body of information, really got after it.

"Upon graduation, we were let loose on the world. Ready to heal. Primed to fight human disease with our massive arsenal of medical knowledge. Knowledge is power, someone has said, and we felt invincible.

"Not long into my practice I was summoned to the hospital emergency room to attend to a man who had just had a heart attack. I rushed to the hospital feeling strong. I was going to save a life! Perform a healing! But after examining my patient I realized I wasn't going to do anything of the sort. The man's heart had ruptured. There was absolutely nothing I could do. No sophisticated procedure mastered in a medical school clinic was worth a dime now. I was helpless to heal. My patient was going to die—and did.

"At that moment I learned just how much I didn't know, a medical lesson not usually taught in school. For all my training and knowledge, the man died. His heart literally broke, and all I could do was idly watch as the muscular pump ceased to perform, as life and breath left him. You cannot know how utterly helpless I felt."

The physician reminded his confidant that one of the major objectives of true learning is recognizing how much we do not know. Any authentic course of inquiry will put the student squarely in touch with her or his limits. The wise listener commented that limitation is a rude awakening for young physicians fresh out of med school—and for other human beings as well. But it surprises us with a most blessed virtue: humility. With humility, we are spared the pangs of omniscience to which we are all tempted. Without perceiving our limitations, we suffer the baser ignorance of being too sure.

We would never have expected it from the sharp, youthful cardiologist. He had learned everything he was supposed to know about heart health, disease, and repair—yet, his patient died. Hurt pride can help character grow. In an emergency room, a physician crossed over a boundary from arrogant optimism to considerate kindness.

Do we expect too much from our society's healers and heroes? That they will always heal and win forever? History teaches us that time is a patient and generous healer. Yet, the sage advice "live one day at a time" is too long a wait for a dying heart patient.[9] A hospital's Wound Care Center got peoples' attention with this blurb: "If it hasn't started healing in a month, it's not healing. It's getting worse."

We must expect change. One skilled in the "art of passing over" anticipates needs and uses resources at hand to sustain life. The Kalahari Desert bushmen of southern Africa bury ostrich eggs filled with water along their journey so that they may be sustained after a hunt on the long trek back home. No bushman takes another's water source, for water means life in the African wasteland.

 THE SURVIVOR IS A HOPE-BEARER where there are reasons for hope and an endurer when hardships refuse to disappear.

The young doctor, above, learned that change happens. It will come! He also gained a few ounces of gumption—practical common sense applied to the puzzling problems of life. That leads us to another pathway for handling transitions.

USE COMMON SENSE

It's not easy to stay "calm and collected" in our highly charged emotional environment. When troublesome situations arise, we may reveal disturbing feelings such as anger, anxiety, distress, denial, depression, even rage. You should be warned: use common sense when facing transitions but don't give away your heart. Our right brain—creative, sensitive, spontaneous self—helps us to respond and to care. But we need the left brain functions, too—deliberateness, purpose, calmness, wise speech, and the ability to solve problems. We get into trouble at the extremes of keeping a stiff upper lip (denial) or insisting on cheerfulness (repression) when wisdom is needed.

Here is a couple, for example, where the wife feels that a different living arrangement is desirable, but her husband's timing doesn't mesh. Let's call them Jane and Bert. Jane presses Bert into looking at developed properties in their city, as well as undeveloped lots. She wins a big round, accomplishes the purchase of a choice building site, and engages an architect in their behalf. While Jane jumps heart first into the project, Bert registers realistic concerns, especially about money matters. When bids are returned and the dream house appears beyond their reach, the customarily cheerful wife becomes agitated and depressed. The architects had become "family." It was a done deal. Then, came Bert's, "Wait. We're going to have to rethink this whole thing." While the couple experienced disappointment, neither of them wished to jeopardize their futures with high costs for property taxes, mortgage payments, and insurance.

Let's put a human face on a different need for common sense. It's Ben Walsh's story. Mildred, his wife, predeceased Ben when she developed hepatitis. He had been the town's Postmaster before retirement, so he had many friends. Ben enjoyed televised sports, played golf, read Western novels, taught a men's Sunday school class at his church, and worshiped regularly with his faith community. But, as a single-again adult, life was incredibly lonely without Mildred.

In time, a female companion entered Ben's life and eased his solitariness. Marge lived nearby and attended the same church as the Walshes. Her husband had died some years before. Ben and Marge enjoyed travel with friends, table games, mealtimes, and quiet conversations. It was on a group bus trip, sponsored by a local bank, when Marge noticed Ben losing his train of thought. His speech became garbled. A careful physical examination revealed an inoperable brain tumor.

"Mr. Walsh has from six months to one year to live," the medical team told his son and daughter who lived elsewhere. Because Ben required assisted living, he was placed in a nursing home. Quietly, the tumor grew and cut short his life. In less than six months following that diagnosis Ben died. His grown children "adopted" Marge into their families and shared her loss, though she and Ben had never married.

Our USAmerica society is getting older in chronological age, but senior adults are getting younger in functional age. Because of genetics, improved medical care, monitored diet, transgenerational product design, and practice of physical fitness regimens, more elderly Americans are independent at ages 65, 75, and 85 than ever before. Health care costs, including Medicare, require common sense wisdom from both clients and health care providers. A combination of social, political, psychological, and moral factors can help reshape society's attitudes toward aging.

In using common sense to achieve goals, a twenty-something couple volunteered for the Peace Corps years ago and served in Eastern Africa. They learned Swahili, acculturated with the Kenyan villagers, and pointed toward a future of Christian missionary endeavor. They learned the wisdom of the extended African family, ways to improvise goods and services, and need for networking with local officials. Now, for more than two decades they have served among the tribes of Kenya as theological educators.

Thus far, we have examined five ways to face change: revisit myth and fantasy, remember biblical heroes and heroines, learn from literature, anticipate the unexpected, and use common sense. Changes do not lock persons uniformly into one place or posture. We respond uniquely according to age, past experiences, temperament, patterns of living and believing, health, supportive resources, and grounds for realistic hope.

Douglas Walrath, professor at Bangor Theological Seminary, writes (emphasis his):

> *When the world changes radically, human beings encounter radically different experiences as they pass through the same developmental stages of life. . . .*(T)hey perceive the same experiences differently from those socialized previously, who are now side by side with them in the same period. . . . They become a "cohort" . . . (i.e.,) contemporaries who share experiences that uniquely and fundamentally shape them. People outside the cohort not only do not share these experiences; they also lack certain basic frames of reference needed to interpret them in the way the cohort interprets them.[10]

Walrath proposes three cohort populations in USAmerica: Strivers, Challengers, and Calculators—according to birth years. Others have proposed categories such as Builders, Baby Boomers, Busters, plus Generation Xers to describe these cohort populations.

Because individuals born in different epochs of history learned to *do* life uniquely, and value things differently, their responses to change, chaos, and challenges are distinctive.

FIND INTERNAL CONNECTIONS

In some of the world's great cities where winters are severe, skyways form elevated pathways for office workers, shoppers, and maintenance personnel. Rochester, New York, for example, averages seventy inches of snowfall each winter. Other cities with heavy snowfalls—Denver, Calgary, Toronto, Montreal, and Minneapolis—have numerous structures linked with skywalks.

They are internal connections between skyscrapers—arteries to the heart of high-rises—permitting people to connect with warm interiors when nature is forbidding.

A landscape designer in Calgary, for example, has created a rainforest-like "world within a world." Locals as well as visitors in winter connect with a warm, artificial environment. Fountains flow, giant ferns grow, rock gardens bloom, and ferns slope toward garden walkways—with snow outside. Sales clerks on break and secretaries from nearby offices brownbag lunch each day and connect in fantasy with a vacation in Samoa, Africa, Hawaii, or the Bahamas. Temperature in the rainforest is thermostatically controlled, so that one enjoys eternal summer even in the bitterest winter. The skyways symbolize complex connections in our lives.

For centuries humankind has relied on gifted persons who have served as linguistic bridges between cultures. Frances Karttunen, a University of Texas linguist, tells the story of some of these remarkable persons in *Between Worlds*.[11] With English now a virtually universal language, we forget that travelers once had to use sign language and pantomime for basic communication with "the others." When Europeans began to explore and colonize the rest of the world, they recruited native speakers as linguistic go-betweens. Karttunen tells the story of a small but most essential subset of the human race—persons able to navigate between their own and the white man's culture.

"For one reason or another, they had already been set apart before they began to speak to outsiders," notes the linguist, " and it was their very isolation that rendered them available and capable of doing the job."[12] Dona Marina, who guided Hernando Cortes through his conquest of Mexico, had been given away by her Aztec parents as a child. In addition to translating for the Spanish conqueror, she bore him a child, the first mestizo, the mixed race stock from which the modern Mexican nation descends. An unusual number of these cultural bridge-builders were women, for example, Dona Marina and Sacajawea, who helped guide Lewis and Clark through their exploration of the American West.

I mention these sensitive individuals because of their gifted capacity to move between worlds. They formed internal connections between the cultures, the present and future. They lived through turbulence and turmoil, without recognition, and opened the future to persons like you and me. It is their gift as go-betweens that we note. We, too, must find the "inside passage" linking one destination to another as we forge ahead with our lives. How do such connections work?

The Chilimacha Indian Nation has roots in southern Louisiana that go back perhaps fifteen to twenty centuries. Small in number, their artifacts appear mostly in USAmerican museums. Their Native American language was preserved on electronic recordings earlier in this century and was cataloged in the Smithsonian Institution in Washington, D. C. Ethnographers today are challenging the Chilimachas to reconnect with their past in order to preserve their future. Linguists have reintroduced their long-forgotten mother tongue to children at the edge of the twenty-first century.

On a visit to the Chilimacha Nation's headquarters, supported through the U.S. National Park Service, my wife and I made an interesting discovery. A couple in their age-thirty transition, with roots in the Louisiana marshlands, had taken up basketweaving in their spare time. They had connections with their grandmothers, now deceased, who had taught them how to weave native baskets from the local cane bark.

Because of our interest as amateur ethnographers and Indian artifact collectors of objects from North and South America, the couple kindly received us into their home. Bill showed us their prize collection of "grandmothers' baskets" with basic artistic designs. Kim's grandmother had taught them as children how to go to the marshes, harvest cane, cut it into needed lengths, strip its bark with their teeth, slice it into uniform widths, keep it in water, dye it as she had done (they used modern dyes, not root dyes), and then weave it into beautiful baskets. Chilimacha baskets grace museums and homes of private collectors.

How did it happen? Bill's and Kim's native American ancestors lived in the south Louisiana wilderness on the fringe of the white man's world. They stepped out of the forests to trade with the Acadians who settled around New Iberia, Clarendon, and Lafayette. Baskets carried their produce and cradled their treasures. Traders bargained for the Indian's artwork. The rudiments of their native culture have become a cornerstone of a new generation.

What do skywalks, linguistic go-betweens, and the native American's way of passing on traditions have in common? They point us to ways we can build bridges to our own dreams by remembering two gifts—the past and the future. We experience transitions while holding in one hand legacies from our forebears and in the other hand promises of the next generations. To connect with past generations and claim heirship with one's own people is the way of wisdom.

The circle of care our creator provides in transitions is not confined to some support group at church or in therapy. It rests in partnership with the generations past and following. Leonard Sweet said, "The decisions we make affect (others), and they have something to say and light to shed about what we are doing and where we are going."[13] Internal connections are what we value— ethical stars by which we navigate life's course. We find internal connections in union with God, the saints, our deceased and living loved ones, and the unborn "others" in generations following.

To summarize, we have constructed a framework for facing change with accountability. Our future is unpredictable. Yet, with pathways marked for us it is manageable—at least for some of us some of the time. But what if we are unable to find our way? How may we get a grip on a world we may be losing? It is to such matters that our thoughts now turn.

REFLECTIVE EXERCISES

For Thought:

1. Can you identify with Christopher Reeve's woundedness? How are you different from the Man of Steel?

2. Have you ever thought of fantasy (a vivid imagination) as a source of power in your life? Is de Mellow correct—that fantasy may provide a way to God?

3. Are there lessons from pathfinders in the Bible that can guide our searchings in today's cultural contexts and events? How?

4. What do you think of a physician who comes to the realization of how much he or she does not know? Have we forced godhood upon frail human care providers?

5. How have you served as a go-between with some person from another culture, generation, gender, or race and the larger human community? Who gave you the courage to care?

For Discussion:

1. Discuss the concept of childhood (or adult) myth and fantasy as a means of coping with some difficult transition in life.

2. Can you recall a psychic or spiritual wound that would not heal—a hurt or failed Dream that required a long time to mend? Are you able to share it with others?

3. Can you recall one *big* idea from reading any kind of literature that has enhanced your ability to manage change?

4. A fateful diagnosis crushes our best hopes of going on with life. Can you share some grand expectation that has been shattered with a broken dream?

5. How has some gifted person helped you to move "between worlds" as you have faced a major change in life? What was the most effective thing he or she did?

NOTES

[1]Christopher Reeve, "The Journey of Christopher Reeve," ABC-TV, *20/20*, interview with Barbara Walters, 29 September 1995; also, 24 May 1996. See film critic Philip Wuntch's review, *The Dallas Morning News*, 30 September 1995, 37A.

[2]*The New Encyclopedia Britannica* (15th ed., 1991) 9:741; and *The New Enclopedia Americana*, International Ed. (1992) 22:693.

[3]Kathleen Arnott, *African Myths and Legends* (New York: Oxford University Press, 1989 paperback).

[4]Anthony de Mello, *Sadhana: A Way to God* (St. Louis MO; The Institute of Jesuit Sources, 1979) 59-60; cited by Leonard Sweet, *Faithquakes* (Nashville TN: Abingdon Press, 1994) 60.

[5]Gail Sheehy, *New Passages: Mapping Your Life Across Time* (New York: Random House, 1995); Jimmy Allen, *Burden of a Secret: A Story of Truth and Mercy in the Face of AIDS* (Nashville TN: Morrings, 1995); James W. Fowler, *Faithful Change: The Personal and Public Challenges of Postmodern Life* (Nashville TN: Abingdon Press, 1996).

[6]Allen, 100-101, 230, 238-48.

[7]William Bennett, *The Book of Virtues* (New York: Simon & Schuster, 1993); also, *The Moral Compass* (New York: Simon & Schuster, 1995). PBS aired its adaptation of Bennett's *The Book of Virtues*, an animated anthology of classic tales and legends offering strong moral lessons for kids, 2-4 Sept 1996.

[8]Charles Foster Johnson, "Learning and Limitation," *The Second Page* (Lubbock TX: Second Baptist Church, 21 June 1994).

[9]Gerald Mann, *When One Day at a Time Is Too Long: Practical Answers to 42 of Life's Toughest Questions* (New York: McCracken Press, 1994).

[10]Douglas Alan Walrath, *Frameworks: Patterns of Living and Believing Today* (New York: Pilgrim Press, 1987) 35.

[11]Frances Karttunen, *Between Worlds* (New Brunswick NJ: Rutgers University Press, 1994).

[12]Frances Karttunen, quoted by Ron Grossman, "The Twain Met Here," *Fort Worth Star-Telegram*, 10 July 1994, C7.

[13]Leonard Sweet, *Faithquakes* (Nashville TN: Abingdon Press, 1994) 165.

Chapter 6

LOSING THE PLACE
WE CALL HOME

Thus far we have learned that even though people take all the right steps, success is not assured. Despite our best efforts, things may not pan out the way we had hoped. Miracles we long for do not happen. God holds them back. For what? For whom? We don't know and we can't see as far into the future as God sees. Of all life's changes, we are most devastated when we lose the place we call home.

 IN HOME LOSS, IT IS NOT WHAT HAPPENS TO US, but our grief work that matters most. Life-changing transitions come from the inside, often after pained and extended reflection.

That has been true in the experience of author and Nobel Peace Prize winner Elie Wiesel. His memoir, *All Rivers Run to the Sea*, is the most recent of his more than thirty books. In it, Wiesel, born in Sighet—a small town in Transylvania that has sometimes belonged to Romania, sometimes to Hungary—recalls being sent to a concentration camp by the Nazis at the age of fifteen.

Now a U.S. citizen and professor of humanities at Boston University, Wiesel tells how the village of Sighet shaped his life. His rich imagination remains entangled with the home of his childhood. In all his novels, it serves as a background and vantage point. In his fantasy, he still lives the memories that formed part of his inner landscape. Sighet was lost, though, when he and his family were swept up by Nazi troops during World War II and transported from their Jewish ghetto to a German concentration camp. The Hungarian gendarmes followed ruthlessly orders to implement Adolf Eichmann's plan for the Jews' extermination.

He hoped the family would stay together, along with their friends. That hope was dashed when they left with the first transport and, a week later, he left with the last. "In the camp," Wiesel remembers, "there were no friends to remind me of my childhood. In the camp I had no more childhood."[1] His remembrances, recorded in his late sixties, tell of a Christian servant woman, Maria, who offered them a safe haven in her remote mountain cabin. His family declined and, with that fateful decision, they lost the place called "home."

Home, like time, is not easy to define. Webster tells us the word *home* comes from the old English *ham* = *village*; akin to the Greek *koiman* = "to still, calm, quiet," literally "to put to sleep." Home is our birthing/launching place—where we start from. While many postmoderns sense no link between God and the gift of life, which we think of as one's self, birth takes us to the core structure of existence. The source of our existence is a unique gift—human and divine—and, therefore, has spiritual significance.

Home is where our heart lies in the formation of identity. Self-awareness is more than tissue and neurochemistry. Home begins with a physical place and a gathering of people whom we prize, or tolerate, or endure. Home imprints us from the start and impacts us all of life's journey. In divine providence, God calls us from "country and kindred," as with Abraham of old, to new beginnings so we may make a home of our own.

Leaving home is not the same as losing one's home. Leaving is natural; it "involves an emotional differentiation from the family where we originated,"[2] as authors Anderson and Mitchell note. Home loss implies that relationships we started with and counted on break up, are "blown away," or deteriorate into attitudes and actions that trap, hurt, or elude us. Not only are family ties laid waste; we no longer have a place to which to return. Such expatriates must learn to live as exiles from their birthing homeland. They forever seek to complete life's incompletes. Home-losers are habitual home-seekers.

 IT IS TO THE TASK OF HOME-WORK that we turn. We need to distinguish what home means today in stories from life—how home may be lost; yet, how home is longed for as a habitat for the heart.

THE INNER MEANING OF HOME

There are a number of ways to get at the notion of home. One way traces the narrative chronicle of at least three homes in one's life span:

(1) Our childhood home with its chances for good and ill. Popular culture abounds with stories of persons who are estranged, cut off, from their families of origin.

(2) Our chosen home or life arrangement by circumstance as marrieds or singles, with or without children, and with all of the obligations that sharing life with another or others brings.

(3) Our covenant home of ultimate value and faith commitment. Faith yields a heavenly home with God and with all true believers of all time—a peaceful place where there is no more separation, no time constraints, no pain, disease, or death. Heaven is a place of unqualified acceptance and joy, meaning not mystery, and of relationships that endure.

Television journalist Diane Sawyer once asked Cuba's Fidel Castro, "Do you believe in heaven and hell?" He appeared stunned, then responded: "No. If there were a God he would not send us to hell." She was insistent, "If there were a heaven, what would you want it to be like?" Fidel replied, "A perfect socialistic state."[3] Sawyer anticipated the Communist leader's anxiety of fate and death. But was his answer doubt or delusion?

While recognizing these chronological ways of viewing homes of birth, choice, chance, and commitment, think with me about your intrinsic sense of *inner home* as well as your heritage, external home. Both one's kept-within interpretation and one's historical family experiences integrate to form the meaning one invests in the concept of home.

The Outward (Obvious) Sense of Home

God wrote home into our very natures (Gen 1–3). If God had not created family life, we would have invented it for ourselves. Community is a part of being human. We enjoy seeing new life spawned on the earth, new generations rising, bringing new hopes and dreams for our tomorrows.

Our personal, environmental home involves awareness of objects and relationships: a geographical location—mountain, valley, city, or village—family, a residence, key events, language, mealtimes, disciplines, tribal lore, holidays, kin folks, a mother's tone of voice, pets, secrets, celebrations, achievements and rewards, winning and losing, hurt feelings, sad partings and glad reunions. We each have come from a tangible birthplace—from the loins of a woman—sired by a man, perhaps aided by genetic engineering. ✱

You may identify with the persuasion of Texas storyteller Tom Dodge:

> There's a strong urge that certain people have—I have it—toward staying put. I guess you feel whatever strength you might have you owe to your family and the land that you grew up in. It would be unthinkable for me to separate from that.[4]

Talk of home translates into memories, thoughts of what might have been, abuse of power, models of courage, having a room of one's own, a desire to feel understood, the need for forgiveness, and fresh starts. As sojourners, we're ever homesick for our true home.

The Inner, More Complex Sense of Home

Our inner home focuses on images of belonging, being loved, feeling secure, staying in touch, sensing our specialness, learning values, caring for one another, and fulfilling our destiny—"The reason I was put here on earth." Our inner home is a place where people meet each other's spiritual, as well as human, needs. Yet, it often remains obscure, mired in complexity.

The interior vision sees exterior things, persons and events, but it sees more. Our inner home is a legacy where sacred energy flows, people fit, and life can be good. When abuse occurs, adversity comes, life turns bitter, health breaks, a job folds, stressors crush, courage waivers, then home can be a shaky place—deep inside as well as outside.

Regrettably, home is the source of some of the worst abuses and evils to attack the human self. Cultic leaders, exploitive parents, senseless siblings who seize their kin for sex play, animal-like fellow prisoners, and sadistic military personnel in isolated patrols can make "hell" of what God intended to be good. When the wounds of abuse, suffering, and diminishment come, we are destined to spend our lives in greater mystery.

inner search for home then becomes
spiritual journey

It is precisely at the point of perplexity where the inner search for home becomes a spiritual journey. Mystery may serve as the birthing place of wisdom, that fertile field from which new possibilities can grow. Life's losses may become thresholds for awareness of the divine Spirit. Eugene Bianchi of Emory University in Atlanta, Georgia, notes that

> to be religious, among other things, is to confront the boundaries of life and death, to grapple with hope and despair, to puzzle over decisions of good, evil, and mixtures of both.[5]

Taking his logic a step further, we who would share life's spiritual journey must walk with people to the edges of the mystery at the heart of their existence. Such encounters open us to transcendent experiences and to knowledge that comes by faith.

 FAITH MUST FIND A RESTING PLACE for the home that lives in our hearts—for relationships tethered to eternity.

LOSING THE SENSE OF "INNER HOME"

Perhaps you know the Genesis story of Abram, renamed Abraham under God's covenant to make him the "ancestor of a multitude of nations" (Gen 17:5).

> The Lord said to Abram, "Go from your country and your kindred and your fathers's house to the land that I will show you. I will make of you a great nation, and I will bless you." . . . So Abram went. (Gen 12:1, 2, 4)

As leaving was right for Abraham, so certain deployments and separations seem right for us. But it is possible for home to get ravaged along the way. Consider some ways home may be lost.

Faulty Parenting and Forming a False Self

Here are excerpts from an open letter by a college student.

> Sir:
> Thank you for the excellent essay "On Being an American Parent" (Dec 15). Oh, how I wish every parent and future parent would read it and take it to heart! . . .
> I love my parents, and I know they love me, but they have ruined my life. . . . I could never tell my parents

anything; it was always "I'm too busy . . . too tired . . . that's not important . . . that's stupid . . . can't you think of better things . . . oh, your friends are wrong . . . they are stupid." As a result, I stopped telling my parents anything. All communications ceased. We never had that very important thing—fun.

Oh, we had love—prompted on my side by an ever-present fear of my mother and pity for my father, and prompted on their side by the thought that I was their responsibility and if I went wrong, they would be punished by God.

What is the result of this excellent upbringing? I'm eighteen years old, drink whenever I get the chance, have smoked pot, and as of a very eventful Thanksgiving vacation, am no longer a virgin. Why? Was it my parents or just me? I'm so very confused—but who can I talk to? Not my parents. My parents could read this and never dream it was their daughter.

I have one important plea for parents. . . . Listen, listen, and listen again. Please, I know the consequences, and I am in Hell.[6]

Potentials for alienation from one's parental home lie all about us from early childhood. A youth's sense of "I" may become blurred with shame, self-doubt, and efforts to hide one's true feelings. Such defenses may give rise to the formation of a false self. A child may tolerate the attitudes, behaviors, and pathologies of family members in order to survive; but, in so doing, is caught in a "doublebind" situation. The true self becomes twisted into covert responses to contradictory parental and sibling initiatives. Developing a false self offers a makeshift strategy for survival, but, sadly, weans an individual from authentic selfhood. Home is cut off in the process of growing up.

 LIFE DISHES UP LESS AND MORE than we deserve.

Parent Loss

Parents may be lost through death, custody battles in court, horrors of war, abuse, abandonment, divorce, imprisonment, or hit-and-run one-night stands between a man and a woman. In my own case, as a nine-year-old in fourth grade, one afternoon an older boy who was delivering newspapers and visiting my school said: "A Mr. Brister was run over today in front of the bank."

I remember thinking, "Oh, God! Don't let that be my daddy!" But it was. It was springtime on the calendar, but it was winter in our hearts as we laid him to rest that day in May. He was cut off before he came all the way through with life. Even then, I felt that so noble a person was too valuable to waste. A quarrel began with the Creator in my childish heart about things that matter. I was flung into the cosmos as a little boy with man-size questions that may be answered only in eternity.

But there are other kinds of parent loss. Entertainer Dick Gregory once told of a schoolteacher taking up money for the community chest at his school. Gregory said the teacher went around the room gathering promises of gifts—of whose daddy would give what. Dick Gregory lied to save face: "My daddy said he would give . . . $15.00."

The teacher turned around and looked mad. "We are collecting this money for you and your kind, Richard Gregory. If your Daddy can give fifteen dollars, you have no business being on relief . . . And furthermore," she said, her nostrils getting big and her lips getting thin and her eyes opening wide, "we know you don't have a daddy."[7]

Dick Gregory started crying. The teacher said, "Sit down, Richard." He confessed, "I walked out of school that day, and for a long time I didn't go back very often. There was shame there."

Broken Dream of Marriage Never Realized

There are almost seven million more adult women then men in the USA.[8] There are just not enough of us to go around for one another. A lovely thirty-eight-year-old woman makes her home with her twin sister. Marla has a master's degree; is a deeply religious person; and loves art, music, and travel. She has a place for "marriage and home" inside, but no man to go with the deep inner space. She is a curator of hope who would enjoy a family of her own. Marla and her twin sister are executive types who may have to create the home of their dreams while adapting to single life. For them, and so many others like them, one is a whole number.

Abuse and Broken Promises

A young man who had been placed by his father in a foster care institution once shared his story. The father promised to come back and get him some day. "I waited seven years for him to come back, but he never came. Something died inside. I never expect to see him again." He was haunted by the fear of being cut off from people who care.

One wonders if there are bridge parents who could help nurture home in someone when hope is starving to death on the inside and birth parents fail. We are reminded of the claim of the psalmist, "If my father and mother forsake me, the Lord will take me up" ("take care of me") (Ps 27:10). The Lord has a lot of homeless children to care for in the earth, and needs help. They are our children, too.

Parental Favoritism and a Lost Blessing

Listen again to this biblical event:

> When Esau heard his father's words, he cried out with an exceedingly great and bitter cry, and said to his father, "Bless me, me also, father!" But he said, "Your brother came deceitfully, and he has taken away your blessing." Esau said, "Is he not rightly named Jacob? For he has supplanted me these two times. He took away my birthright; and look, now he has taken away my blessing." Then he said, "Have you not reserved a blessing for me?" Isaac answered Esau, "I have already made him your lord, and I have given him all his brothers for servants, and with grain and wine I have sustained him. What then can I do for you, my son?" Esau said to his father, "Have you only one blessing, father? Bless me, me also, father." And Esau lifted up his voice and wept. (Gen 27:34-38)

People carry invisible wounds into adulthood from early experiences of feeling second best; wearing hand-me-downs; being compared critically to an older or younger, high-achieving brother or sister; being told that one is too tall, short, thin, or fat; or being chosen last for some event or game at school.

The *blessing*, in the biblical sense, is the power to advance the family line—potency, possessions, privileges, and property—with all others in the clan taking second place to, usually, the eldest son who was blessed by the father. The elder brother in

Jesus' story of the prodigal son (Luke 15) illustrates powerfully what happens when one feels odd-person-out, unfairness, unappreciated, or where the party of life passes one by. Home goes helter-skelter with the blessed child into a far country. Home is enveloped in old hatreds, burning jealousies, and death wishes to be rid of the favored child.

Poor Health
Involuntary Career Termination
Forced Retirement

Take the case of a chaplain who moved from Chicago to a Southern city. He accepted a position in a large, church-related hospital. He opted to lead a clinical pastoral education program in that hospital with a twenty-seven-year-old administrator who accused him of insubordination and terminated the veteran chaplain.

At about the same time, the man's wife had a tumor requiring surgery. Eventually, she experienced a stroke that left a blood mass in her brain. The ending of his work and loss of his wife's health required him to be "out of the job loop" for more than a year. While at home physically, the man's sacred sense of home was severely threatened.

Unwelcome Presence of "Outsiders"

A friend from Northern Ireland related how the unplanned, intrusive presence of a guest had disrupted his family's existence.

> The person was related to us; yet, not close to us. She stayed too long . . . about six months. Dorothy and I lost our sense of intimacy, privacy, even our identity as a couple. It has taken us a long time to renew our covenant.

You may recall Robert Frost's poem, "The Death of the Hired Man," in which a conversation occurs between Mary and her husband Warren. Warren has been to the market and returned with household items. Mary tells him that old Silas, the man who helped them with haying through the years and has been gone so long, has shown up on their doorstep.

Warren is not sympathetic. He feels that Silas is worn out and is back just to put upon them. Silas had "nothing to look backward to with pride, and nothing to look forward to with hope." Mary speaks softly with a woman's tenderness, "Warren, he has come home to die: you needn't be afraid he'll leave you this time."

idea that home is a place of grace

"Home," Warren mocked. Then he described it as a kind of birthright. ["Home is the place where, when you have to go there, they have to take you in."] Mary saw home in different terms, as a place of grace. "I should have said it's something you somehow haven't to deserve." Home is there for us by virtue of our existence.

Mary insisted that Warren go check on Silas who came back to them broken and ill. They were the only heart and soul he knew. Warren returned with one word: "Dead," was all he answered.[9]

boundaries

[Frost's poignant picture of the need for home, anger over unwanted intrusion, and the difficulty of offering home to the homeless is a study in the need for boundaries and privacy. ["The Death of a Hired Man" is a metaphor for all the lonely people who try to go home again, who feel the darkness, who hear the howling of the dogs and the gate creaking in the wind at night, and hope that family and friends will "be there" for them.

Intrusiveness is not just the "outsider" who wants in. It may be a his-hers-ours marital arrangement, following double divorces and remarriage, where three sets of children are present. They are there; yet, are not really insiders. They are each related to an adult in the family circle; yet, they have different bloodlines, different genes, perhaps different last names. The family can be "at table" but triangled in spirit.

What's to happen with a boomeranger son or daughter who doesn't make it in the big city or who divorces a spouse and shows up back at home? Equally difficult is the what-to-do-with-mother quandary after an aging father dies. If she moves in, will she be an intruder with a couple or a healthy addition as the "resident in-law?"

Infidelity

Unfaithfulness through adultery is all about us. In one USAmerica survey, one out of four evangelical ministers who responded said they had had intercourse with someone other than their spouse. Sixteen percent of the pastors refused to answer the question.[10]

When a young wife discovered her husband was sexually involved with another woman, she at first denied it. She loved him. She did not want to discuss the terror she was feeling as he tore away from her and went into another woman's arms. Her lover is now her enemy. She has sued him for divorce and seeks to be both career mom and home mom for their two children. Home is very painful for her. Romance is shattered. Security is elusive. The management of her limited time, energy, and financial resources is maddening.

Infidelity is more than a matter of physical, sexual failure. It is a matter of betrayed trust, broken promises, disregard for the other's needs, dishonesty of living a lie, and a destructive climate robbed of true intimacy. When the most intimate bond known to a man and a woman has been destroyed in another's bed, integrity, compassion, and devotion are already dying.

Cutting Off Parents or Eluding Each Other

A religiously devout mother confided, "I have two children who do not speak to each other. We can't ever get together as a family, so I visit them separately." The family's children are now adults. They continue to demean one another at great cost. The woman and her husband travel a lot. When they return to the place that should be home, it is not there. The family cannot gather about the hearth or table at any holiday. Their inner home is robbed of joy and ravaged by grief.

Little Sense of the Tragic

A person who has been hurt, perhaps hardened, by divorce may respond to life events in an unpredictable, even harshly inappropriate manner. Such was the case with a physician friend who is a highly successful, sophisticated specialist, but who was damaged by divorce. A graduate from New York University, his corrosive spirit oozes acidity.

Once, as we spoke of heavily populated regions of planet Earth, he said:

> Those people multiply like rats. Best they kill each other off
> to save overpopulating the planet. Any relief sent their way is
> no better than throwing it into the ocean.

Bitterness is in, and blessedness is out with this man, still caught up in swirling emotions from a broken marriage.

Consider another context. The president of an institution came under a corporate restructuring mandate. Bright, in his early thirties, the new CEO reorganized the structure and systems from the top down. Most members of the organization sensed their careers being damaged under his leadership. His harshness led to a rash of of resignations. In commenting on his new leader's management style, a staffer said: "Don has no sense of the tragic. He says he wants what's best for us, but he doesn't really care." Such dehumanizing tactics contributed to employees' feelings of inner home loss.

Without sensing its tragic forecast of future trouble, a Michigan judge ordered a three-year-old-girl taken from her college-student mother because the woman had put her child into day care.[11] Circuit judge Raymond Cashen said the girl's father deserves custody because his own mother, a homemaker, had promised to take care of her. A lovely child, thingafied by court order, will grow up in a world of conflict.

When the significance of life's tragic dimension fails, a twenty-six-year-old Playboy starlet can marry an eighty-nine-year-old attorney, worth $400 million. Is there enough glue in such wealth to hold a disparate couple together for a durable marriage? What do such selfish, calculated arrangements say about the worth of human personality? How can kingdom of God family ties endure with so little evidence of a lasting home?

In these ways and more—self-destructive behavior, confused sexual orientation, abuse by cultic gurus, toxic ruptures in religious organizations, conservative/liberal political power wars, and switching from one career to another—one's inner sense of home may be lost.

THE DYNAMICS OF INNER HOME LOSS

 IN FACING TRANSITIONS OF INNER HOME LOSS, we must attend to grief work, then move beyond it to embrace the unknown future.

Loss of home requires attention not only from the grieving person but from all individuals in the orbits of that one's life. Grief obliterates landmarks; it blinds one's eyes to immediate sources of care. Grieving persons hang on to signs and symbols of lost objects, lost persons, and broken dreams: a letter, a newspaper clipping, a lock of hair, a photograph, a pair of shoes, a half-empty bottle of perfume, a man's wallet, an art object, a piece of jewelry, a used Bible, old kitchen ware, a forgotten flower folded into a book.

Grief gets out two cups for coffee in the morning, but only one partner is left. It sits in a lonely room and talks to an empty chair of a lost love object, as though the person is there. Grief calls the person by name and imagines that they hear, understand, love back, and are O.K. somewhere.

You may recall the love story of Sheldon Vanauken and Jean, whom he called "Davy." Their love crossed oceans and was bound up in the search for faith. Through the ministry of their mentor and friend, C. S. Lewis, at Oxford, their love became transformed by the presence of Christ. Davy was struck by a mysterious illness and died slowly. Vanauken described their last meeting one night at the hospital thus:

> They prayed together that God might lighten their darkness and by His great mercy defend them from the perils and dangers of the night. Then he said, "Davy—I love you forever." She whispered: "Oh, my dearest!" He stroked her hand, and she said in a strong voice: "Oh God, take me." They knew that she was dying. He said: "Go under the Love, dearling. Go under the Mercy." And she said: "Amen. Thank you blessed dearling."
>
> He placed the wedding ring that had been removed from her fingers when they became so thin back on her ring finger and repeated a vow: "With this ring I thee wed . . . for all eternity." Later he wrote, "I shall not know this side of eternity how much she knew. Her last words were: 'Oh, dearling, look.' "[12]

In time he took her ashes out into the snow, opened the box and scattered the ashes using the sower's motion. Later he wrote, "When I had done, the flakes were coming down hard. I left the rose on the old cross. I said aloud: 'Go under the Mercy.' "[13] He did the only sensible thing under the circumstances. The proper attitude toward such a loss is mourning.

Grief work tackles the immediate duties of a hundred little things that must be done. Bills must be paid. "Thank you" notes must be written. The void of the lonely nights must be tolerated; and bereavement dreams must be survived. We who know the inner meaning of home must know how bitter it is to lose it, whatever the reason.

Grief has a way of isolating us. A career-changer has no job; an amputee has no arm. Suddenly, belongers become outcasts. People who care for persons facing transitions not only stand by the door and wait at work, at church, at military chapels, in industrial offices, and hospital suites. We must enter the doors where folks search for meaning and long for healing of their invisible wounds. Wisdom discovers grief's healing balm in numerous ways: divine care, empowering friendships, recompensed justice for evil, therapeutic endeavor, and the healing passage of time. Still, wistfulness lingers. One's search for inner home may last a lifetime. ✳

THE SEARCH FOR INNER HOME

There was once a teenaged boy—adopted years before by well-intended, childless folk—who was obsessed with the notion of finding his birth parents. Who were those people that in an ancient era may have set him out to die? Why did they let him go? Would they be sorry now? If they could, would they "put him up" for adoption again, or might they want him back?

The search for home went on for years. It aggravated his legal parents. "Walter seems so mixed up," they said. All the world's lost children look for a permanent home, too.

Postmoderns living in a technoculture of violence and environmental risk have discovered, willy-nilly, that their home is leaving them. All that our forebears assured us would be there forever—the land, Sears and Roebuck, Social Security, Medicare, and AT&T—are going the way of all flesh. We don't like it—living flip-flop, like aliens "in the land promised" us.

Could it be that all our losses—all our griefs—have a promising intent? Are we like ancient Abraham to "search for a city with firm foundations, whose architect and builder is God" (Heb 11: 8-10, NEB)? Is Jesus Christ truly our sacrificial Savior who helps divinize all our losses? In the very act of searching by faith for our lost inner home we embrace the diminishments life brings and contribute to the betterment of the world. In the words of Teilhard de Chardin:

> If Christ is to take possession of all my life . . . then it is essential that I grow in him not only by means of . . . suffering . . ., but also by means of everything that my existence brings with it of positive effort.[14]

Hope in God turns family destruction upside down. Instead of dead weight, our "momentary affliction is preparing us for an eternal weight of glory beyond all measure" (2 Cor 4:17). It is as though inner home loss serves as a catalyst for transformation of one's personality and a consequent worldly vocation of greater value. We turn now to future story possibilities in our struggle to regain a sense of "inner home."

REFLECTIVE EXERCISES

For Thought:

1. Draw a line across a clean page and mark it with five-year intervals. Imagine it as your lifeline graph. Place an X for your age; an O for your hoped-for life expectancy.

2. Using the lifeline graph and readings here, how old were you when major transitions began? Recall one such event.

3. What mistakes in handling the loss of "inner home" would you like to avoid?

4. Recall one key loss in your life narrative that has shaken you to the depths. What have you done about it?

5. In Teilhard's terms, have your sufferings brought with them anything of "positive effort?" How is your past hurt shaping your future story?

For Discussion:

1. Etchings of Elie Wiesel's memoir were freighted with brokenness, disruptions, and loss. Yet, valuable lessons emerged. Has that been true for you?

2. How does a single person interpret his or her destiny as a home-maker? Does one's intent to marry make a difference in doing home-work as a single person?

3. What happens to one's inner sense of home in learning that one's spouse is gay? How does a person come to terms with such a turn of events?

4. Can one's story be reinterpreted in light of seeing the hand of God's providence in a particular event? How?

5. What do you expect to happen next in light of your life narrative? Will there be a happy ending in your future?

NOTES

[1]Elie Wiesel, *All Rivers Run to the Sea* (New York: Alfred A. Knopf, Inc., 1995); see, Wiesel, "The Decision," *Parade Magazine*, 27 August 1995, 4-6. [Note: The idea for this and the next chapter was sparked by reading of lectures at the C. G. Jung Institute, Zurich, Switzerland, 28 June–9 July 1993, by Kathrin Asper-Bruggisser, Ph.D. The author's treatment of the inner home idea here is entirely his own.]

[2]Herbert Anderson and Kenneth R. Mitchell, *Leaving Home* (Louisville KY: Westminster/John Knox Press, 1993) 25.

[3]Fidel Castro, ABC-TV "Prime Time Live," 4 March 1993.

[4]Tom Dodge, quoted in Thomas Korosec, "Down-Home Delivery," *Fort Worth Star-Telegram*, 28 February 1993, F1, 5.

[5]Eugene C. Bianchi, *Aging as a Spiritual Journey* (New York: Crossroad, 1982) 177.

[6]"A College Student," *Time*, 22 December 1968, quoted in Robert A. Raines, *Soundings* (New York: Harper & Row, 1970) 35.

[7]Ibid., 94-95.

[8]*The World Almanac and Book of Facts* 1994 (Mahwah NJ: Funk and Wagnalls, 1994) 363. For elaboration, see James N. Lapsley, *Renewal in Late Life Through Pastoral Counseling* (Mahwah NJ: Paulist Press, 1992); Sharon R. Kaufman, *The Ageless Self: Sources of Meaning in Late Life* (Madison WI: The University of Wisconsin Press, 1986); and Leonard Sweet's discussion of AgeQuakes in *Faithquakes*, 147-66.

[9]Robert Frost, *Complete Poems of Robert Frost* (New York: Holt, Rinehart, Winston, Inc., 1958) 49-55 (emphasis supplied).

[10]Archibald Hart, "Life of the Pioneer Pastor," Leadership Network: Church in the 21st Century Conference, 14-17 June 1992, Las Colinas TX.

[11]"Custody Controversy," *The Dallas Morning News*, 27 July 1994, 1-A, 5A.

[12]Sheldon Vanauken, *A Severe Mercy* (San Francisco: Harper & Row, 1977) 157-77.

[13]Ibid., 177.

[14]Teilhard de Chardin, *The Divine Millieu* (New York: Harper & Row, 1960) 67.

Chapter 7

THE STRUGGLE
TO BE HOME AT LAST

The American novelist James Mitchner wrote in *Hawaii* that it is an awesome time when people experience the death of their gods. He referred to missionaries who sought to wean Pacific islanders from traditional religion and offer them one true God. Deities who had inspired the Hawaiians' hopes and fired their imaginations for centuries were called into question. In the process, the islanders lost their bearings. Such profound change is experienced as loss. Even when good is gained, loss will be mourned. One of our most difficult tasks is leaving old life structures in order to move on to new ones.

The loss of our sense of "inner home" is akin to the death of the Hawaiians' gods. Such a passing over is not the rite of leaving home in young adulthood. Rather, it is the devastation caused when home leaves us in hurtful ways—abandonment by a parent, substance abuse, emotional disorders, custody battles, acts of violence, health matters, broken covenants, and criminal behaviors. You may recall the Genesis story of how Adam and Eve forfeited the Garden of Eden. The havoc and ruin of that first home loss through disobedience has receded into forgetfulness. Still, the human race lost the possibility of entering a perfect "garden" again on this earth.

 WITH THE GARDEN DESECRATED, we each live east of Eden and search for ways past the flaming sword and cherubim guardians, through the gates of Paradise.

In our journey of soul crafting, driven and distracted, spiritual reality may get pushed to the edge of awareness. It isn't intentional. The possibility of deepgrounding—true connectedness to ourselves and others, to history and nature, ultimately to God— eludes us mid the manic press of life. Signposts pointing toward

our *essential home* (our true place in the cosmic order) fade mid
the nitty-gritty of fast traffic and the daily grind. Wade Clark Roof,
California sociologist of religion, has said 37% of mid-aged
Americans he surveyed are religious seekers, but have no title to
a spiritual home.[1] His study shows a top item on the human
agenda is peace with God and seeking a place the Bible calls "a
better country." Our task is to heighten that vision for people
who've lost their way, yet who live with spiritual concerns.

To help seekers become citizens, we need to understand basic
family systems concepts; to learn from ordinary peoples' stories;
to devise metaphors that put home first; and, finally, to show
people the way "home." First, some assumptions about family
systems theory.

SOME ASSUMPTIONS ABOUT FAMILY SYSTEMS

Generations Matter

Long before meeting and hearing the late Murray Bowen of the
Georgetown University Medical School faculty, I appreciated his
insights about family systems.[2] A classic Freudian psychiatrist,
Bowen changed over time—in part as he sought to go home again
and get in touch with his family of origin.

Impressed with intergenerational influences in his own family,
Bowen introduced his psychiatry residents to the genogram,
"family tree" concept, devised originally by researchers at
Harvard University. The goal of family therapy, whichever system
one elects—from Salvador Minuchin's "structural therapy" to Carl
Whitaker's "experiential therapy"—is new interactions between
family members, not insight alone.[3] Rather than a designated
patient requiring extended psychotherapy, the entire family is
engaged by a caregiver and taught how to discover home—to
change and grow.

 FROM A SYSTEMS POINT OF VIEW, all family members are intercon-
nected, so the way one person behaves affects all other family
members.

Vital Connections

What storyteller Robert Bly calls "the long bag we drag behind us"
is actually one's repressed shadow or disowned self. We must
come to terms with all the angers, deceptions, shameful feelings,

and failed relationships stuffed into our self-bags during childhood and adolescence. "We spend our life until we're twenty deciding what parts of ourself to put into the bag," wrote Bly, "and we spend the rest of our lives trying to get them out again."[4] For Bly, Robert Louis Stevenson's tale, *Dr. Jekyll and Mr. Hyde*, is the story of Everyperson. We are walking contradictions of good and evil.

Family systems theorists go beyond Bly and hold that a symptom is connected to the system. Where do one's sexuality, wildness, impulsiveness, anger, passivity, lack of boundaries, or potential for violence originate? In some sort of family or family surrogate—just as do one's capacity for kindness, integrity, commitment, faith, hope, and love. Getting parts of oneself "out of the bag" of one's developmental history is an individual clients' job in traditional psychotherapy, whereas regaining one's sense of "inner home" in family systems theory is a group endeavor.

A family systems therapist must connect with an entire family's desire to change *and* its resistance to change. Mastering resistance is hard detective work: teasing out displaced aggression, exposing triangles, countering challenges to the therapist's competence, noting blame, and confronting denial.[5] The client's question becomes, not "What's wrong with me?" but "Who are my people? How may I leave, yet relate to, my family of origin? What is my true place?"

Complex Behaviors

In one's search for "inner home," linear thinking must yield to circular causes, events, and circumstances. *A* does not always lead to *B* and on to *C* in cases of child molestation or abandonment, for example. A stepfather arrested in Dallas for leaving four children home alone, while his wife went to a neighboring state to purchase a car, was not prepared for parenthood in the first place. The stepfather functioned more like an immature child than a responsible parent.

Family events are more like marbles in a pinball machine than like markings on a ruler's edge. Incidents such as sexual abuse, which appear as "effects," are also "causes" of other episodes. For example, Woody Allen was accused of sexually abusing his seven-year-old stepdaughter while leaving his wife, Mia Farrow, after twenty years of marriage. But there's a twist. He claimed love for Mia's twenty-two-year-old adopted daughter. Intervention in such a complex cycle, not merely treating a so-called identified patient, is required.

Seeking Wholeness

Homeostasis—the restoration of equilibrium among members of a family system—is not the equivalent of regaining one's sense of "inner home." (The term *inner home*, as it is used here, implies a habitat for the heart.) It is a secure sense of place in time, but it is more than that. It has a grip on eternity—an ultimate connection with God. The Greeks called one's inner home "immortality of the soul"; whereas, Christian believers link our potential for salvation to resurrection of the body. Faith affirms that such durability of the human spirit is the ultimate goal of existence (Phil 3:10-11).

(For our purposes, the concept of an inner home is both a present reality and a future hope.) It incorporates key elements of salvation, for example, "peace with God" and what the apostle Paul described as "fruit of the Spirit" (Rom 5:1-11; Gal 5:13-26). Inner home connects us in healthy ways with other family members, yet holds to clear boundaries of self-definition (Bowen's differentiation of the self).[6] (One's inner home is neither enmeshed, with lost boundaries, nor disengaged from one's family members.) An "at home" person lives within appropriate bounds of affiliation, respect, and care across gender and generational lines.

A PERSON WELL ESTABLISHED "AT HOME" takes up life's tasks with determination, courage, humility, hope, and grace.

A New Way of "Being"

A woman who, in her early thirties, had experienced what her North Carolina psychotherapist called a "nervous breakdown," eventually came to see that crisis as a breakthrough. Married to a college professor and mother of a young son, Millie Howe had a great heap of grief hidden inside her. Millie was orphaned by her father's death at the fateful Oedipal age of seven. She was cut short from working through her attachment to her father by his premature death. For a girl, the term is *Electra complex* or situation, not Oedipus complex, as in a boy's case.

In Freudian thought, such a girl not only feels a possessive love for her father but antagonism for her mother as a rival for his affections. As an adolescent, ideally a young woman experiences

[handwritten margin note: inner home is both a present reality & a future hope]

her father as a trusted male figure and source of security. In time, her parent identification is healthfully transferred to heterosexual pursuits and object attachments.

Millie was unable to come all the way through with a healthy resolution of her intrafamily relations. She was terribly jealous of and competitive with her only brother, Jim, who was two years her senior. During her age-thirty transition, Millie emotionally "cut off" her mother and brother.

In exploring her loss of relationships—her sense of home—with a wise therapist, Millie learned her brother had suffered even greater losses than she had. She came to see that death and developmental issues, not Jim and her mother, were her real protagonists. Such forces were much more complicated to address than her feud with Jim and her mother alone. All three of them were drawn into the extended systemic therapy process. Though resilient, they each will carry some emotional scar tissue the rest of the journey.

This story has a serendipitous twist. With their thinking oriented to "true home" vision, Millie, Jim, and their widowed mother became sensitized to other persons in sticky family situations. They discovered a truth advanced by the late Swiss psychotherapist Carl Jung. Ideally, the recovering "patient" himself or herself becomes a healer.

Before pursing further how one may regain or help other persons regain the sense of "inner home," a caveat. We sometimes forget that one is a whole number. Singles count as families, too. Families need not be nuclear to function effectively. This is especially true with single-parent issues. As Carolyn Bohler noted, "Some 'single' people like to consider themselves families of one, while others consider themselves as members of a friendship-family-network."[7] We are talking about millions of USAmerican households. Singles include persons who expect to marry someday and also widowed, separated, and divorced individuals.

Singles include formerly married persons with or without children, well-positioned career people who do not desire marriage, and retirees who may or may not contemplate marriage. Around 35,000,000 USAmerican households are headed by single adults. Many of them are struggling to find a secure place called "home."

We turn from these basic assumptions to an incident that informs how one may regain a sense of "inner home."

A STORY THAT POINTS THE WAY

The destruction of the Berlin Wall in 1990 brought visions of the end of Nazism and Communism. People who gathered at the broken wall saved bits and pieces of that awful barrier that had snaked its way 100 kilometers across the face of Berlin.

Earlier, my family and I visited Berlin and explored the wall's west perspective. We learned about deaths of would-be escapees from East Berlin and saw curtains held in mortared, bricked-up windows, as private houses blended into the wall. A baby carriage was suspended in barbed wire at one point—telltale evidence of some East German parent who tried to escape but failed. That visit into East Berlin through "Checkpoint Charlie" was a memorable experience.

Old enemies tend to have long memories. Yet, reconciliations happen. A remarkable meeting occurred in Nuremberg, Germany, site of war crimes trials of Nazi officials after the Second World War.[8] A psychiatrist from Harvard Medical School sponsored an "Operation Understanding" meeting between middle-aged offspring of Nazi military officers and Gestapo agents and Jewish adult children of Holocaust survivors.

We think of Hitler's attempt to exterminate the Jews as a horror—6,000,000 persons lost—herded onto trains, stripped of their privacy and possessions, forced into concentration camps, then gassed and burned in death camp ovens. Family members were separated from their houses and from each other in a loss that will renew itself over and over as long as one asks, "What is humankind's ultimate capacity for cruelty?"

For the heirs of the generation that produced the Nazis and Holocaust survivors the question becomes more personal, "What am I?" The Nuremberg participants, with German names such as Erika and Jewish names as simple as Nathan, sought ways out of their ironic sense of history. With discipline, honesty, courage, and restraint, these aliens to one another faced their old hatreds, anxieties, and lost sense of home. Would-be victims do not rest easily alongside would-be exterminators. Life-and-death struggles, long buried under mountains of ashes, walked out of death camp stories.

In one touching scene, a Jewish son of a Holocaust survivor embraced the daughter of a Nazi killer. Her father had overseen the very camp in which some of his relatives had died. She got in touch with her father's awful deeds in order to lay them aside. He celebrated the infinite worth of the experience of just being alive.

What an eventful week that was. "They did not come to forgive and forget," commented the TV reporter, "but to better understand events and forces in their lives."

The connectional experiences at Nuremberg were an attempt to regain a sense of fatherland and motherland. Such efforts at human understanding emphasize, as James N. Lapsley puts it, "the relational character of the self, both to other persons and to a 'third,' who ultimately is God."[9]

"But what does a happening in Nuremberg, in 1993, have to do with me?" you ask. Precisely this. <u>Forgiveness experienced</u> leads to <u>home rediscovered</u>. A sensitive caregiver may assist home-losers and home-seekers to a fuller, more accurate perception of their true dwelling place. A symbolic place, linked to the horrors of Holocaust, provided exiles and displaced persons a link with their native soil. In order to find such a pathway home, we may use picture language.

THE USE OF METAPHORS AS SIGNPOSTS

As with "Id, Ego, and Superego" in Freudian therapy and "cultural archetypes" in Jungian theory, "<u>inner home</u>" is a construct for <u>the self-in-relationship.</u> Lapsley affirms,

> The self refers to the felt <u>sense of ownness and sameness</u> that a person perceives, together with their connections below the surface of awareness, and sometimes to disconnected fragments below the surface.[10]

For example, when the alienated prodigal son came to himself in Jesus' story of the Waiting Father, he remembered home. There, even hired hands had plenty to eat (Luke 15:11-32). The youth's developing self incorporated as "self-objects" his father, a man of wealth and power; perhaps his mother, for her ideals and good taste; and his older brother, for his narcissism and jealousy. This self-in-relationship I call the sense of "inner home."

Life was reframed for the lost son when he determined to return to his father's house as a servant, not a rebel. He would repent, confess his sin against heaven and home, then cast himself upon his father's mercy. Little did he imagine the warm

[margin handwriting: inner-home's a construct for the self-in-relationship]

Home is more a relationship than a physical spot

welcome and celebration that lay in store. Home in this sense is more of a relationship than a physical spot. Going home is more than a journey. It is renewing the covenant of belonging to God and to one's people for all of life's seasons. The at-home self is both a point and a process.

In a modern parable of family triangles, therapist Stephen Lerner, of the Menninger Foundation in Topeka, Kansas, has scripted and produced a screenplay titled *Going Home*.[11] Eileen, a young woman in a midwestern city desires a new level of relationship with her aging father who is now a heart patient. She flies "out" from her own husband, Bob, and daughter, Nicole, in order to relate directly with her father.

Upon arriving at her parents' home, her overfunctioning, perfectionistic mother takes charge. Her passive father fades into the furnishings of each room. With much urging, she gets him to go for a walk and helps him connect with his own father's premature death when he was only eight. The destructive triangle devised by her mother years before to cut Eileen off from her dad is exposed. Her attempts to detriange and reframe her relationship with her dad are only partly successful, but lessons from the disconnected fragments of her past help Eileen relate better with daughter Nicole, and with her disengaged husband, Bob.

 IN COUNSELING, THERAPISTS MAY USE METAPHORS intentionally to describe family predicaments and help persons communicate when words fail.

To a woman whose son and daughter were estranged from her and from one another, a counselor spoke of siblings who "poison each others' wells." A recovering addict spoke of being "reborn." A gay man's father came out-of-the-closet, which he called "a secret," and accepted his son without approving his sexual orientation.

Family therapist Peggy Papp, of the Ackerman Institute for Family Therapy, uses a technique she calls, "couples choreography," both to make a tentative diagnosis about a couple's relationship pattern and to observe what progress has been made as counseling proceeds.[12] The husband of one couple with which Papp used her fantasy dancers approach "saw his wife as a fleeting person in a fog—a disappearing phantom. He would try to follow her and capture her but she was always just out of his reach."[13]

In contrast, the wife saw her husband "as a 200-pound rock" whom she wanted transformed into a soft flower.

In pursuing their mutual fantasies at the conclusion of their sessions, Peggy Papp noted "his and hers" fantasies. He saw them on a beach enveloped in the rhythmic motion of the waves. She saw them like two balloons tied together in a park one sunny, windy day. They were free-floating, bobbing up and down with the wind, but at least they were tied together. Given this background and use of story and metaphor, how may we rediscover and help other persons find a sense of inner home?

HELPING PERSONS FIND "INNER HOME"

We never go back, exactly, to where we were before some change and transition uproots us from familiar territory. We have to go forward, face issues of substance, and make hard choices. You can make a difference by attending to key issues in your own or another person's or family's spiritual journey.

 LET'S EXPLORE SOME WAYS TO HELP persons find "inner home."

Focus on Identity Issues

Our identity is tied to gender, age, nationality, language, relationships, customs, role functions, vocation, religious persuasion, our status in society, and lifestyle. When any *thing* happens to the essential components of one's identity, our inner region gets shaky. When child, or job, or spouse, or health, or house, or sense of safety, or familiar governance is lost, one's identity shifts. We help persons adapt to life change by feeling their pain with them, helping them name the experience or "put a face" on what is happening, inventorying available resources, and building on their ego strengths. The transition lies in who one is becoming.

Face Failed Expectations

Ross Goldstein, a San Francisco psychologist and author of *Fortysomething,* reminds us how easy it is for our midyears' laden ship to run aground. Goldstein comments,

> The three big wake-up calls of midlife are disconcerting. They include the realizations that, one, you're not going to become president of the company (or, if you are president,

it's not as much fun as you thought it would be); two, your
family is never going to look like Ozzie and Harriet's; and
three, you're not going to live forever.[14]

Such painful realizations can prompt persons to new levels of
growth. We all do soul-crafting in midlife; we think about making
key changes and reorganizing our priorities.

Put Garbage Where It Belongs

Chefs and nature lovers know that the shortest distance between
rubbish and a fresh start is the compost pile. People with a
passion for tomorrow have to unload yesterday's junk and today's
burdens. We've described a lot of pain, hurt, and loss. Saying
goodbye to all that hurts or is unworthy of our focused attention
is not easy. According to Goldstein,

> Saying goodbye to an unrealistic image of yourself, to your
> dreams that haven't panned out, to careers, to people—
> friends, spouses, parents—inherently carries pain. But
> you've got to say goodbye before you can say hello to what-
> ever will be the next life structure that you're looking at.[15]

If a person can't let go of pain and risk the future, that
individual will likely repeat old mistakes and stay stuck in old
patterns. Putting hurts and pains of this-and-that experience on
the compost pile fosters forgiveness and new growth. Such action
says God has something better in future store.

Treat Unhealed Wounds

A professional friend conferred with a physician and a businessman, both of whom fear change and face an eroding sense of
security. The businessman's fortunes are changing; new competitors are on the scene. After ten years of being in charge, his
financial foundations collapsed, and he declared bankruptcy. The
doctor dumped displaced aggression onto their confidant, who
sensed the physician's real enemy is growth of managed health
care in this country. Both men live with unhealed wounds that
affect their daily work. Loss of career status may lead to loss of
home.

WHAT DO WOUNDS THAT WILL NOT HEAL do to our at-homeness?

Pastoral counselor Bill Ratliff noted,

Unhealed areas from the past affect the way we live in the present. When we are having difficulty dealing with a transition, even after we have worked on it, we may wonder if some hurt from our past is mixed in the problem.[16]

For example, a middle-aged father may have difficulty disciplining his preteen son, not because of the boy's behavior, but because the dad has unresolved issues with authority figures. He and his own father may never have come to closure on disciplinary matters. Now, his son's behavior opens an unhealed wound.

Both father and son must learn that boundaries are not mere rules. They are guidelines for safety and essential for healthy communication and action. Healthy home life encourages the empowerment of self-directed, internal authority.

Nurture the Spirit

People's passion, will, and heart are at work in family issues: when communication fails, when a cardiac-defective child is born, when a spouse faces cancer, when a dad has a heart attack, when a son commits suicide. The world may not seem like a just place. Doubts and questions often lead folks to ask why God acts this or that way, why something has happened, or does anyone care? One anguished father protested, "Life isn't fair!" At such times, people need the Lord.

The poet Wordsworth wrote, "We come from God, who is our home." At life's end we return to God. There's a lot of talk these days about "bonding" in marriage and parenting, that mysterious melding of two persons who love each other as dearly as life itself. Our ultimate bond is with the Lord of creation. The apostle Paul said it well: "Your life is hidden with Christ in God" (Col 3:3). With divine strength we need not lose heart.

 LEARNING TO LISTEN TO GOD while we pass through some painful transition is not easy.

We often confuse our own desires, hurts, dreams, and longings for a new beginning with God's purposes. Like the Jews in Jesus' day, we want to see a miracle—the supernatural, big time. But, as Elijah the prophet learned, God's voice is often gentle as a whisper, rather than like an earthquake or raging fire (1 Kgs 19:12). The Spirit's call to fresh vision, to move forward with life, confirms our own inner yearnings for new beginnings. We learn assuredly that home is our heart's desire.

Live the Mystery

There is a delicate mystery in inner home life. We will not always have companions and planet Earth (Matt 22:30). God calls us away from any idolatrous dependence upon and worship of one another. Faith invites us into a transcendent union "with Christ in God" and with all those who have gone before us.

How may we know that we and persons we cherish are on the way home?

NO PLACE LIKE HOME

Patterns of our lives are altered continually by shifting events: a child leaves home, a spouse abandons marriage, a family is deployed on assignment across the country, a national leader is assassinated, refugees forsake their homeland, or a widow buries her mate and lives alone with a legacy of memories. But relationships do not die when separations occur. Home takes on an identity of its own as we experience change, yet go on living with memories and hope.

Occasionally, a "savior figure" arises on history's stage to hold a family together or to keep a tribe, nation, or empire from disintegrating. Vi Hilbert, a seventy-six-year-old Upper Skagit elder from the Puget Sound region, has given much of her life to preserve her Lushootseed native language. Working from translations and transcriptions of the histories, stories, and songs of her people, she puts the ancient words into her computer. The language savior's house sits on a hill above the Duwamish River valley, near Seattle, Washington. Twice divorced, married a third time for almost fifty years, Vi Hilbert has a native sense of home.

> I am the only child of two traditional people who expected me to carry on their work and the work of their ancestors. To meet that obligation, I've been attempting to leave as much as I can for coming generations.[17]

Ms. Hilbert believes that creating this legacy fulfills her destiny.

For her work, Vi Hilbert was named one of eleven National Heritage Fellows by the National Endowment for the Arts. While she will have a place in the folk-art hall of fame in Washington D.C., many unsung heroes and heroines make home as an enduring legacy for others on the journey.

Going home is suffused with mystery. There is so much we don't understand, mid all the joy/pain and love/fear of all the years together. We are ever venturing, risking, stumbling, and rising to move on in home ties. In some respects we never arrive; we are always on the way toward homeness.

According to John Killinger, the task of "going home" involves placing "ourselves in the mystical presence" of God who fills "all our days with beauty and meaning."[18] We begin to feel at home with ourselves, all of "the others," with nature and history, when we are at peace with God. There comes a season in our lives of wisdom for the journey's difficulties and gratitude for its blessings. We are encouraged to believe that "whether we live or whether we die, we are the Lord's" (Rom 14:8).

In summary, home is a place "we haven't to deserve." It is a love story from first to last with work, devotion, wisdom, joy, and kindness as the secret ingredients. Faith guarantees our home forever, when God is in it from beginning to end. In the words of John Killinger, "What was of the earth becomes almost entirely of the Spirit, until at last we enter into God and (God) becomes all in all."[19] When we experience deep peace—with self, God, and others—we are home at last.

REFLECTIVE EXERCISES

For Thought:

1. Comment on the idea that while we may not feel "at home," we are always searching for homeness.

2. Family therapists speak of enmeshment keeping a person trapped in dysfunctional circumstances. How can you break out of old patterns of family hurt?

3. Sometimes, the way home is a "far country" experience—divorce, a substance-abuse treatment center, prison experience, or other such pathway. What of your personal "far country" experience? Is home nearer or farther away now?

4. When people change, they think of loss—of giving up something. But regaining one's sense of "inner home" implies reaching a goal, or adding someone or something to life. What innovations or new insights have come your way?

5. The New Testament apostle Paul spoke paradoxically of "counting loss as gain." What might you lose (give up) in order to gain your dream?

For Discussion:

1. Discuss with your accountability partner or share group the fact that people cannot manage change unless they have a dependable inner core of identity and integrity (character).

2. Comment on the notion that the concept of "inner home" is both a present reality and a future hope.

3. How would you explain the author's concept of "inner home"? How do you connect with the "inner home" idea?

4. Given the Holocaust survivor narrative here, how significant is forgiveness in our struggle for community?

5. Take a metaphor from art, nature, music, literature, or your own experience and use it to tell what is going on right now in your own family narrative (e.g., a triangle.

NOTES

[1]Wade Clark Roof, *A Generation of Seekers* (San Francisco: Harper San Francisco, 1993) 8, 63-88.

[2]Murray Bowen, M.D., *Family Therapy in Clinical Practice* (New York: Jason Arounson, 1978).

[3]Carolyn J. Bohler, "Essential Elements of Family System Approaches to Pastoral Counseling," in *Clinical Handbook of Pastoral Counseling*, vol. 1, expanded edition, ed. Robert J. Wicks, Richard D. Parsons, and Donald Capps (Mahwah NJ: Paulist Press, 1993) 595.

[4]Robert Bly, "The Long Bag We Drag Behind Us," in *Meeting the Shadow: The Hidden Power of the Dark Side of Human Nature*, ed. Jeremiah Abrams and Connie Zweig (Los Angeles: Jeremy P. Tarcher, Inc., 1991) 7.

[5]Carol M. Anderson and Susan Stewart, *Mastering Resistance: A Practical Guide to Family Therapy* (New York: Guilford Press, 1983).

[6]Bowen, 529-48. Also, Ken Hemphill's "Kingdom Family Relationships," in *The Antioch Effect* (Nashville TN: Broadman & Holman, 1994) 103-28.

[7]Bohler, 610. See Carolyn A. Koons and Michael J. Anthony, *Single Adult Passages* (Grand Rapids MI: Baker Book House, 1991).

[8]Reported on *Dateline*, NBC-TV, 16 March 1993, Jane Pauley, hostess.

[9]James N. Lapsley, *Renewal in Late Life Through Pastoral Counseling* (Mahwah NJ: Paulist Press, 1992) 33.

[10]Ibid.

[11]Stephen Lerner, *Going Home: A Family Systems View of Change*, videotape (Topeka KA: Menninger Foundation).

[12]Peggy Papp, *The Process of Change* (New York: Guilford Press, 1983) 142-64.

[13]Quoted in Bohler, 593.

[14]Ross Goldstein, *Fortysomething* (Los Angeles: Jeremy P. Tarcher, 1990), quoted in Prevention, April 1993, 54.

[15]Ibid., 57.

[16]J. Bill Ratliff, *When You Are Facing Change* (Louisville KY: Westminster/John Knox Press, 1989) 37.

[17]Marsha King, "The Language Savior," Seattle Times, copied in *The Dallas Morning News*, 27 July 1994, 5-6C.

[18]John Killinger, *Christ and the Seasons of Marriage* (Nashville TN: Broadman Press, 1987) 61.

[19]Ibid., 62. See Calvin Miller, *A Covenant for All Seasons: The Marriage Journey* (Wheaton IL: Harold Shaw Publishers, 1995).

Chapter 8

TAKING RESPONSIBILITY
FOR YOUR LIFE

The passages described thus far have taken many complexities flooding our lives into account. _Flooding_ describes dreadful feelings of being swamped, out-of-control. Soul crafting, we have noted, endures shifts, inspires plans, and opens us to future stories. Life anticipates more from us than complaints, defensiveness, and stonewalling. We are shapers of, as well as being formed by, historic events. People who care employ both providence and perseverance—faith and work—in pursuing what James Fowler calls "the personal and public challenges of postmodern life."[1]

Confidence that life continues beyond this earthly frame makes a great deal of difference in the way we _do_ life now. When you recite the Apostles' Creed and proclaim assurance in "the life everlasting," you introduce the dynamic of hope. The empowerment hope brings to life changes everything.[2] Hopers can face the reality of a new day, find energy for work ahead, challenge forces of evil and injustice, discover strength in community, and remain faithful in the face of discouragement. Persons of faith are motivated to try, to care, to persist, to forgive, and to remain vigilant in facing life's realities.

 EXPLORING DEPTH DIMENSIONS OF MEANING in human experience reminds us that all of life may become potentially sacred.

Anthropologist Sharon Kaufman's interviews with sixty older Americans moved her beyond stereotypes to more accurate ideas about persons who take responsibility for life. Strength of character obviously guided the varied passages of her respondents.[3] Along with their challenges and life chances, an idealized picture of what life might be was reflected in her interviewees' self-definitions. Her observations about "life plans" and value directedness parallel my own findings.

Healthy mapmakers desire meaning and passion to go forward with life. We want the strength to go on. Are there proven pathways to keep us on track? A basic step is mustering the courage to go forward with life's mission.

THE COURAGE TO GO FORWARD

Ancient wisdom literature describes the way we should live in order to achieve life's objectives. "The path of the righteous is like the light of dawn, which shines brighter and brighter until full day" (Prov 4:18). This representation of the life course for a wise person is a luminous pathway, suffused with light midst mystery's shadows. The sage's advice points to feet that do not stumble despite life's adversities, and to tranquility in contrast to the dark path and anxious "stuckness" of evil persons.

The "path of the dawning light" theme appears in experiences of Roberto and Celi Britto, of Rio de Janeiro, Brazil. The mid-fifties couple have impacted their home city through their caring vocations and those of their children. Upon completing their advanced degrees in theology and education, respectively, Roberto and Celi began career tasks in Rio a quarter century ago. Their self-reports of growth, change, and consolidation of identity inspire our own courage.

Roberto has worked through four occupations: pastor of a Christian congregation, chaplain and clinical pastoral educator in a large hospital, theological educator, and, today, he is a clinically trained psychologist. Celi is academic administrator of Colégio Batista Shepard, a K–12 private school with a student body numbered in the thousands. Along with their successful careers, they have parented three gifted children. The eldest, a physician son, practices psychiatry in Rio; the middle child, a girl, performs internationally with a choral-dancing group; and their younger daughter plans to become a lawyer.

After his parents' separation, as a child, Roberto moved with his mother and sister from a small city to a great metropolis. There was no male model in the home. Rather than becoming embittered, he took up the task of offering healing to persons torn asunder by family betrayal, poor communication, and conflict. Celi dedicates her giftedness as an educational administrator to helping her students achieve life's best.

We sense Roberto's courage in a message to his former teacher and mentor.

> I still bring with me—and have shared with many others—the marks of a ministry which is dialogical, contextualized, and redemptive! I thank God I have learned that from you, both in words and example.

The Brittos' stories of idealism, achievement, and hope-filled leadership in their native Brazil can inspire others who wish to master life's transitions.

 CHANGE HAPPENS. The transitions that follow changes are inevitable. Transitions come, not merely in clear-cut endings, but in feelings of ferment that one is in some sort of change process.

MASTERING TRANSITIONS

Mastering transitions is an unending challenge—whether for individuals, families, institutions, political parties, businesses, cultures, or nations. In relation to time, change may be characterized as fast—like a forest fire raging uncontrolled along the California coast, a terrorist bomb attack, or a couple's instant death in an automobile accident. Change may also be viewed as a slow, evolutionary process. Slow transformations may be seen in the shifting structures of the independent states of the former Soviet Union; the decline of monarchies in lands such as Nepal, Swaziland, Sweden, the Netherlands, and Great Britain; or a person's slow death with AIDS or Alzheimer's disease.

Managing the transition's tempo depends on one's perception of what's happening, degree of involvement in the process, its surprise or anticipated nature, and one's own adaptive resources. Transitions differ when it's us or them.

The diagnosis of a brain tumor for Michael H. Walsh, Tenneco's late chairman, shocked his peers. One of America's most respected CEOs, Walsh held the philosophy that to win trust, a leader must practice openness and candor. What appeared to his diagnosticians as "serious but treatable brain cancer" proved them wrong. Walsh's destiny spun out of control. In a short while, he was dead. For family and close friends, his loss was more than a statistic. Mike Walsh symbolized the leading edge of organizational empowerment.

Transitions are personal; yet, they are not solitary experiences. Here is a ninety-year-old woman who, long ago, entered "the ageless years." She reaches for an indefinite future in slow motion. Her life is a challenging process with diminishing options. Ellen's needs are webbed to those of all the other residents in her retirement center, to millions of senior USAmericans, and to providers for their care. Health, courage, faith, and supportive caregivers are her prized assets.

Mastering transitions depends on the perspective one brings to any change event, as well as one's resources for facing it. Viewers of the identical event will respond to it differently, according to their involvement level, emotional stability, and spiritual maturity.

One's perception of the tragic explosion of the *Challenger* spacecraft, when seven astronauts lost their lives, was shaped by one's relationship to NASA, to parts manufacturers of O-rings, to flight crew members, as well as by one's trust in God and in ground crew operations. Family members of the lost space flyers have contributed valuable models of courage, grief management, spiritual strength, and concern for coming generations in appropriate memorials to the victims.

When Dave Leestma—a three-time space shuttle pilot who has logged more than 500 hours in space—speaks, people listen. "As you get ready for a shuttle flight, especially your first one," Leestma recounts, "the one thing astronauts are all aware of is the risk you take."[4] A man of deep religious faith, he read reassuringly from God's Word two days before his first flight, October 3, 1984: "Do not be afraid of sudden panic, . . . for the Lord will be your confidence" (Prov 3:25-26). Leestma said he received real peace from that promise; he and his colleagues had a good flight. He flew on two more shuttle missions in 1989 and 1992.

Managing transitions can go another way. A gifted educator at age sixty-seven faced retirement ahead. He steeled himself for changes at work, scheduled annual physical examinations, and planned for secure housing with his spouse of forty-plus years. He authored essays about the aging process. But, when the time of formal retirement arrived, Howard Mullen (who knew all the right answers for others) plunged into serious depression. He found it difficult to employ the faith and help he had advocated for fellow retirees for himself.

ONE OF THE MOST HOPEFUL BENEFITS OF FAITH lies in the avenues it opens for facing a larger reality.

FACING REALITY

Each of us faces wake-up calls in our own way. There is no single change agenda that works for all of us. Knee-jerk reactions are a common practice. A discovery approach offers the safest pathway through change. We each have to find and face reality for ourselves. Still, there are many would-be guides around with platitudes and prescriptions.

Cal Thomas, of the *Los Angeles Times*, describes "the media gods" who deliver "the truth" to USAmerica in black-and-white terms. Because "bad" news makes better news for some reports than "good" news, reality often suffers a negative drag. We are drawn to the bizarre. A nation's leader is assassinated by a radical extremist; forest fires burn thousands of acres of timber in a Western state; a fifty-six-year-old executive is forced out of work by company downsizing; a couple is killed in a freakish auto accident near Cape Girardeau, Missouri; or a mid-fifties killer of his twenty-two-year-old, live-in girlfriend, stuffed her body into a barrel, caulked it shut, then called his deed "an accident." We live in a can-you-top-this culture in which televised video games and thriller movies merge surrealism into virtual reality.

In a more positive vein, how are fellow Americans facing reality? Having visited the relocation site of a Christian congregation in Colorado, guests were impressed with pastor Del Hampton's remarks at a groundbreaking service:

> Our church has come to a place of its crossing over. Had we chosen not to cross over, then we would have chosen to wander around in a future of futility without the blessings that God would shower upon us. You and I need to grow. God has planted us here, and while we're planted here, we need to grow and bloom.[5]

Two visionary couples helped to make the congregation's reality possible. One gave the valuable site; the second couple networked with volunteer builders. A new building was being constructed several miles away on a prime location. Many delays had been faced when one couple, part-time residents, paved the way for the "place of crossing over." They arranged for a team of volunteer craftpersons to complete the construction. The transition had taken years, but it seemed to occur in one mighty effort.

Facing reality is more than a cliché. It happens every day in the lives of people all around us. Following a national election, *Time* magazine editor Strobe Talbott transitioned into an ambassador-at-large slot in a new presidential administration. Talbott is a specialist on Russia and the other states of the former U.S.S.R. He learned the Russian language early, majored in Russian literature at Yale, and wrote a master's thesis on that subject as a Rhodes scholar at Oxford University.

In addition to translating and editing two volumes of Khrushchev's memoirs, Talbott has written five books on the relationship between the U.S. and the Soviet Union. That the president, his friend from twenty-four years earlier at Oxford, needed him as a special adviser to the Secretary of State on the new independent states, impressed the reporter. Talbott crossed over to the other side after twenty-two years as a journalist.

"This is a bolt out of the blue," he reflected. "I never expected to be in government, never aspired to be in government. It's a classic example of an offer I could not refuse."[6] Facing reality builds on the solid foundation of years of good work for Strobe Talbott. Without his extensive education in Russian language, history, and literature; journalistic expertise and publications at the highest levels; the offer would not have been his to accept.

Hebrew scripture is replete with stories in which God's people "crossed over" to new challenges and opportunities. Hear God's promise to a rising Israelite leader, Joshua, after Moses' death. It serves as an enduring reminder that reality must be viewed through eyes of faith.

> Be strong and courageous; for you shall put this people in possession of the land that I swore to their ancestors to give them. Only be strong and very courageous, being careful to act in accordance with all the law that my servant Moses commanded you; do not turn from it to the right hand or to the left. . . . Then you shall make your way prosperous, and then you shall be successful. . . . Be strong and courageous; do not be frightened or dismayed, for the Lord your God is with you wherever you go. (Josh 1:6-9)

The threefold call for courage and spiritual stamina, ethical instruction, and command to lead Israel into the promised land is accompanied with a promise of God's presence and blessing into the unknown future.

 "BUT HOW DOES ONE GRASP REALITY as a resource today?"

Take a leaf from the notebook of a Christian marriage ceremony. The bride is an American citizen from Kansas City, Missouri. The groom is a native of Paris, France. They had met years earlier when the bride studied and taught school in France. An American marriage was arranged, with a wedding party of parents, relatives, and friends of the bride. It paralleled a wedding in France, celebrated at another time, which included the groom's friends.

The USAmerican ceremony featured contributions from the bride's sister and brother-in-law, residents of New Haven, Connecticut.[7] Rhythms of praise, prayer, and promises marked the celebration of their covenant-making. The centerpiece of the worship service was a group reading of Psalm 100 by all four of the couples' parents. It anchored each of the participants and gathered friends in a larger reality: "The Lord is good; his steadfast love endures forever, and his faithfulness to all generations" (v. 5).

The water is wide between Missouri, U.S.A., the bride's ancestral home, and Paris, France, where she and her husband will make their home. The "tie that binds their hearts in Christian love" is the Spirit of God, whom they trust as their redeemer. That couple has found the Center—the eternal light of love within.

 IN SEARCHING FOR THE STRENGTH TO GO ON, we often wonder how to chart and map life's course. We must know where we have been in order to know where we are going.

MARKING LIFE'S CHANGES

We are each trekkers on a course through time and space. Were you to live to be eighty years of age, you would survive some 30,000 rotations of planet Earth around the sun. Cultures shaped by pragmatism of the West are so activistic that we have few ways of marking key moments in our lives. Once a year on July 4, USAmericans pause to remember how we became who we are.

Every four years, we gear up for a presidential election and inauguration.

A pilgrimage one family made to Oberammergau, in Bavaria, southwest of Munich, Germany, introduced them to people who take time to mark life events. Each ten years, local citizens produce the passion play depicting scenes connected with the crucifixion of Jesus Christ. The dramatic representation keeps a promise made centuries before by their ancestors who were protected by a mighty act of God. The rhythm of life in that unique city is marked off history's calendar in decades. How different life's pace is there in contrast to residents' timing on the island of Maui, Hawaii, awaiting the next eruption of Haleakala's volcanic crater!

Is it possible to become ghettoized in our high-tech culture so that we overlook rites of passage marking life's key changes? Beyond Bar Mitzvah, in which a Jewish lad is recognized for reaching the age of religious duty (usually his thirteenth birthday), how do postmoderns mark key events in a person's life?

Custom anticipates gifts at high school commencements, and gifts plus a reception for a couple following the exchange of their wedding vows. But who recognizes the ins-and-outs of all the other mutations in peoples' lives: experiencing adolescence, a first driver's license, college graduation, a broken engagement, the birth of children, a miscarriage, a move into a new apartment or to a different city, job transfer, divorce, facing cancer, getting fired from work, placing a loved one in a nursing home, sponsoring an estate sale, or the "silent passage" through menopause?

 SOME SO-CALLED "SIMPLE" CULTURES have found ways to mark life's passages. Upon close examination such cultures are characterized by profound complexity.

On a mission to the East African nation of Kenya, it was possible for my family and our hosts to witness a Maasai tribal celebration. We had traveled northwest from Nairobi via an escarpment, descended into the great Rift Valley, entered the Narok District, then twisted and turned into a mountain fastness where the elusive Maasai lived in their mud-floored kraal huts. It so happened that we arrived during the celebration of a large group of young warriors' (technically named *moran*) return from the wilderness. These young men had been cast together as age-mates from their earliest years and had been bonded in the ritual act of circumcision. Already well trained in the lore of clan and cattle—their main economic resource—they had been initiated as moran. The third life stage of initiation, the rite of junior elder at about age thirty, was at hand.

According to anthropologists Amin, Willetts, and Eames, studying the ways of Maasai males during their years as age-set moran, the warriors live as one body of brothers. No one is permitted to eat or sleep alone. Their residences in the *manyatta* form a close grouping of huts, "each of which is a large barrack-room for a full band of moran, plus their mothers and girlfriends"[8] The compound of the manyatta is a wide-open area for walking about, talking and dancing, which, with courtship, are the main diversions of the warriors. In earlier days, the moran had to show personal bravery by participating in a lion hunt and kill (now forbidden by law).

On the particular day of our visit, a festive occasion was underway. A large number of age-set morans had just returned to the kraal for rites of passage from young warrior status into junior eldership. Their bodies were elaborately finger-painted with red ochre, which dried like tattoos on their shiny ebony skin. Their hair was massaged with ochre. They each carried a *rungu* club or spear, symbolizing their prowess and skill as hunters.

The prancing, parading warriors passed in line before us. Some of the young women joined part of the parade. Children clung to their mothers' skirts. Movements were punctuated with a rhythmic chant that sounded like "Ooooooh-yah . . . Oooooo-yah." The returned warriors took turns with high standing jumps, hurling bodies upward while grasping tightly a *rungu* club or spear. Lines of ochre-colored bodies moved across the mountain meadows in loose formation. Their lunges, yells, and movements appeared part of an ancient ritual. From that day forward and for years to come, the moran would be junior elders in the tribe and caretakers of herds of cattle.

A Maasai warrior knows who he is and what time it is in his life. His place has been marked out in an arduous process of selection and elimination. His status in the *manyatta* and later as junior elder is fixed.

Initiation rites for Maasai women are much simpler and of a briefer nature. A girl of thirteen years traditionally undergoes the rite of female circumcision. Usually performed by an older woman specialized in wielding a razor blade, the clitoris is removed—

sometimes the labia as well—in an operation that "makes a child a woman."[9] Many observers consider this one of the worst ongoing abuses of women in the world. The young woman's head is shaved, and she is allowed to marry through a social contract, arranged by her parents with clan members and representatives of the future husband's family. The man's family usually pays a *labola* (bride-price) in cattle to the woman's father. A couple might be wed in a simple ceremony, or with an elaborate wedding ritual and great feast for the entire community.

Once a marriage is consummated, the woman's chief duty is conceiving, birthing, and caring for her offspring—along with pre-dawn milking of cattle and evening collection of firewood. The only time she misses those routine chores is during pregnancy. Life is both simple and hard in the Maasai kraal.

 THE MAASAI RITUALS underscore how sources of meaning stand out in some societies and how stages along the way are well marked.

Life for Westeners may be marked by negatives, such as "So many years since . . ." an accident, destructive storm, job loss, terrible fire, or loved one's death. More joyous events should be remembered: beginning a business or professional practice, a new job, a silver wedding anniversary, or birth of a child. Such markings pass to future generations a legacy for tomorrow.

THE GIFT OF TOMORROW

 THE STRENGTH TO CHANGE lies in cultivating courage, taking risks, practicing faith, using discernment, and "marking the trail" for future generations.

But where do we get the "stuff" to survive life's wake-up calls, to cradle bold visions and make fresh starts? You have been challenged to awareness of what is going on inside you, along with noting historic and cultural shifts around you. According to George Barna, persons with whom you rub shoulders on a daily basis

> are desperately seeking the keys that will unlock the secrets to achieve significance in life and bring them greater fulfill-ment. . . . Comparatively few have arrived at what is deemed to be a reasonable or satisfying conclusion.[10]

We have seen that the code that unlocks the secrets resides in spiritual empowerment. Also, networking opens us to dynamic interaction with others. We are not clever or wise enough alone to manage all that life brings.

We have been encouraged to learn the art of transitioning God's way. In one of his last conversations with his friends, Jesus said, "It is to your advantage that I go away, for if I do not go away, the Advocate will not come to you; but if I go, I will send him to you" (John 16:7). Grasp the significance of Jesus' transformation plan. Robert Raines described it this way:

> By a creative withdrawal of himself, Jesus allowed the Spirit to abide in us always and everywhere as comforter, guide, companion. God trusts us enough to leave us alone in this world, in the (power of the) Spirit.[11]

 WE MUST CULTIVATE THE ART OF "BEING ABSENT" from the familiar if we are to obtain the gift of change.

In a real sense, God's dearest gift to us is himself, the ultimate pathfinder. We call that gift "grace." Amazing grace awaits us in both the special and mundane events of life.

In navigating the journey, our survival gear is not for ourselves alone. We must prepare the way in behalf of the generations following for issues they will face: ethnic diversity and racial unrest, economic uncertainty, medical ethical issues, power of the media in decision-making, challenges to family values, violence, crime and gun control, gambling's rising pricetag, gender and sexuality issues, an aging population, provision for health care, environmental concerns, and world peace.

In summary, we have reached deep into the roots of our cultural and religious history to find means for facing life's transitions. We have looked at worlds beyond and learned from strangers on distant shores. We have sought and found wisdom from wise persons across the ages.

The naturalist John Muir once said: "When one tugs at a single thing in nature, one finds it attached to the rest of the world." The investment we make in change-work and transition-work is not for ourselves alone. It is attached to "the rest of the world." When we tug at our own personal issues, a larger vision looms. Generations yet unborn depend upon our care for earth's "family"—home, community, business, the media, industry, technology, government, and cultures in all the lands of earth. As future-crafters, may we build well.

REFLECTIVE EXERCISES

For Thought:

1. How are your transitions different from those your parents faced? Is there less or more to look forward to? Why?

2. In commenting about his closeness/distance to his father, a man said: "I feel real ambivalence about my father's death." How do you manage boundaries between yourself and others in your family? In your workplace?

3. Was a psychiatrist right who said, "All of us have . . . unspoken sin in our lives . . . and so we tend to identify with someone who has been apprehended for something sinful or wrongful?" Whatever became of sin?

4. If you could control your destiny, what would you change at once?

5. Imagine writing your future story today. What would be the core plot for narrating your own future?

For Discussion:

1. How are "the sufferings of this present time" related to hope for the "glory about to be revealed to us" someday (Rom 8:18)? What does that biblical promise mean?

2. How may we encourage one another in times of struggle that hurt and baffle us?

3. Are there rituals filled with meaning in your experience that may be passed on to future generations? Share or illustrate a ritual that made some transition meaningful.

4. Putting ideas into practice is what this book is all about. Talk about some ways to put faith and hope to work in your life.

5. What "thread" are you tugging at now (John Muir) that appears attached to a larger world?

NOTES

[1]James Fowler, *Faithful Change: The Personal and Public Challenges of Life* (Nashville TN: Abingdon Press, 1996).

[2]See Andrew D. Lester, *Hope in Pastoral Care and Counseling* (Louisville KY: Westminster/John Knox Press, 1995) 138-52.

[3]Sharon R. Kaufman, *The Ageless Self: Sources of Meaning in Late Life* (Madison WI: University of Wisconsin Press, 1986) 166-67, cites the work of Robert A. LeVine, "Adulthood among the Gusii of Kenya," in *Themes of Work and Love in Adulthood*, N. J. Smelser and E. H. Erikson, eds. [1980]. "By 'life plan,' I mean a people's collective representation of the life-course viewed as an organized system of shared ideals about how life should be lived and shared expectancies about how lives are lived. My assumption is that every people has a life plan in this sense—it is the normative aspect of their culture viewed from the perspective of the individual—though it is elaborated as explicit ideology in some cultures and not in others" (p. 82).

[4]David Leestna, "500 Hours in Space . . .," *Louisiana Baptist Message*, 28 July 1994, 11.

[5]Del Hampton, *Mountain Valley News*, republished in Rocky Mountain Baptist, June 1994, 13.

[6]Strobe Talbott, "From the Managing Editor," *Time*, 1 Feb 1993, 12.

[7]Unpublished order of worship, *In Celebration of Marriage*, uniting Julia Ferguson and Jerome Dutilloy, Midwestern Baptist Theological Seminary, Kansas City, Missouri (30 July 1994).

[8]Mohamed Amin, Duncan Willetts, and John Eames, *The Last of the Maasai* (Nairobi, Kenya: Westland Sundries, Ltd., 1987) 83.

[9]Ibid., 166. Female circumcision is frowned upon by many women across the world's cultures. It is seen as dehumanizing.

[10]George Barna, *Absolute Confusion* (Ventura CA: Regal Books, 1994) 13.

[11]Robert A. Raines, *The Gift of Tomorrow* (Nashville TN: Abingdon Press, 1984) 35.

EXPLORING
RITUALS OF TRANSITION

During the season of sending and receiving greetings for Christmas and the new year, it is a ritual of long standing at our house to enclose a friendship letter with our greeting cards. A letter is focused spirit. Its message conveys greetings to friends in faraway places. Our words become deeds by noting: "We are together in spirit though far apart."

Rites of friendship often take the form of a visit, a meal with symbolic table setting or seasonal decor, sharing of photographs taken during a visit, a periodic get-together of friends, a group cruise or trip to some favorite part of the country or world, a professional meeting with colleagues, or a birthday or anniversary party with tokens of remembrance and joy.

In writing your life narrative, part of what may be missing is ritualization of experience. I noted in chapter 8 our lack of rites of passage and rituals of meaning for epochs in modern life. Mythologist Joseph Campbell wrote in *The Hero with a Thousand Faces* that the purpose of rituals is to help move people through difficult transitions and challenging times of transformation. With sensitivity for the lack of meaningful rituals to mark shifts in our life course, suggestions appear here to prompt your own creativity. Innovative readers will devise novel ways to celebrate special events or mark rocky pathways. We need rituals in order to tell our stories and to imagine what the future narrative of life will be like.

Let's consider what rituals might mean in life's passages, and then illustrate rites appropriate for various events on life's journey.

THE WORLD OF RITUAL EXPERIENCE

I once heard of a family's pilgrimage to the Wailing Wall, in Jerusalem, in order to experience profoundly their son's bar mitzvah. The ceremony of a thirteen-year-old boy's passing over from childhood to religious duty and growing adolescent responsibility was celebrated in Israel. Rather than initiate him in their homeland, the family went to considerable expense to recognize that nodal transition in its history.

In caring for persons from birth to death, many Western parents, ministers, physicians, educators, and politicians lack rituals of passage and rites of remembrance. What, for example, goes along with a teenager's new driver's license (beyond increased insurance)? How shall we remember a "pink slip" from one's job or a marriage interrupted with divorce? We each know the pain of endings. One of my desires here is to illustrate ceremonies for marking life's changes in a desacralized culture.

Biblical personalities understood the power of ritualized experienced. They "marked trial" long before native American Indian ceremonies in order to move people across major thresholds of transformation. When we consider practices such as circumcision, altar building, health laws requiring days of purification, sacrificial sin offerings, feasts and festivals, fallow sabbath years for the land, marriage rites, funeral occasions with special burial sites, the digging of wells, laying on hands of blessing, coronation of kings and queens, dedication of buildings such as the temple, and symbolic peacemaking by the exchange of gifts in Old Testament lore, we note how deeply rooted rituals are in Hebrew scriptures.

Jesus Christ was steeped in Jewish tradition. He understood ritualization and symbols that endure in human societies. Appreciating the value of signposts that point the way to human change and growth, Jesus provided baptism and communion (the Lord's Supper or Eucharist) as enduring reminders for all Christendom. "As often as you eat this bread and drink this cup" are words pointing people to God in many religious traditions, lands, and languages. Baptism for a new believer is more than a pious habit. It marks a powerful, life-transforming change of direction, attitude, and identification with a community of faith. Such rituals point persons to a glad future in an ultimate "promised land."

A ritual does not mean putting on our smiley faces and arming ourselves against more hurts, wounds, and disappointments. Rather, such experiences are soulwork, shared with others, marked by both memory and hope. The postmodern West has laid aside the intuitive traditions of more "primitive societies" and followed the logic of Enlightenment thinking. Beyond ceremonies of religious confirmation, marriage, and the funeral, have we not lost our way in transitions management?

 FEW MEANS ARE PROVIDED IN WESTERN CULTURES to act out the glad events and sad ordeals of life.

HOW RITUALS EMBRACE CHANGE

Crafters of transitions seldom appear on history's horizon. The late anthropologist Arnold Van Gennep noted in *Rites of Passage* that ritual is society's mirror, reflecting endings and beginnings, separation and reunion, and death and rebirth. Rituals for thousands of years have lent humankind ways to tend the human spirit, mark events, identify with one's people, and claim a future. Consider how rituals work.

Tending the Human Spirit

Rituals reenergize us for life's next step. The stories we have read of passages—personal, family, community, national, or global—involve unsettling events, disorientations, and waiting for the future. Observances of blessings, parting, healing, growing old, changing locales, marriage, or becoming a citizen of a new land can nurture the human spirit. Angers may subside. Healing happens. Vows change. Purposes grow. Values embolden. Directions are set. All this because tradition provided a way and one's community cared.

Marking an Event

Rituals encourage acts of recognition and remembrance by marking a particular event in a person's, family's, or group's life. Achieving school graduation, getting a first driver's license, becoming married, having a child, losing a job, or retiring—life's passages are chapters in a story. Taking a small gift or a map or a list of professional resource persons to the home of someone who has recently moved into one's city is a celebrative deed. It is a ritual act of welcoming a newcomer. It is not the move, but an expression of caring that one has left one place and is writing a future story elsewhere.

Identifying with One's People

Cultural anthropology teaches us the value of belonging to one's group. I live in a city where law enforcement officials have identified more than 200 gangs. Belonging involves some ritual exploit of initiation, often a violent feat such as a drive-by shooting. Rites of identification—for example, inductions into a sorority or fraternity or into a branch of military service—address and seek answers to the question, "Who are my people?" They tell of one's heritage and homeland, language and people, cultic practices and connections. Initiation rites symbolize one's familial, educational, occupational, national, or military identity as a badge or uniform is donned.

Claiming the Future

Rites of passage pass the torch to the next-comers. A burial puts away the earthly remains of a loved one, friend, or community figure. But the memorial words and solemn occasion do much more than end things. They open one to a support community, to a next step, and to a fresh start on the journey. Rituals help us stake out a claim on tomorrow while remembering yesterday. Special ceremonies help us see life's significance in a new light, appreciate the past, and frame a future story for days ahead.

 LET'S CONSIDER SOME WAYS RITUALS MAY HELP persons face life's transitions in our own time.

RITUALS OF SUSTAINABILITY

A university graduate moving from Tallahassee, Florida to a job in Chicago might wish a blessing for her new apartment—even with rented furnishings. Shifting life's narrative from the sunny South to a cold (in many ways) climate requires a sense of security. She needs a way to assure her safety, support, and sustenance in a new environment. A lintel blessing near a door or window, a group prayer or candle lighting ceremony could buttress her life.

One is supported in times of transformation by letting go of some things and holding on to others. In selling their home of more than thirty years, Jim and Billie (see chapter 1)—along with their minister, family, and neighbors—could have framed their deed of trust. They may have taken a plant or tree from their former homesite and planted it in a small garden area at the retirement center. They could have burned their dated insurance policy or the paid-off mortgage paper, shredded it, or released it into the wind. They were braced somewhat by moving treasured art objects and favorite furnishings into their new habitat. All was not forsaken.

What of the person in an eldercare center who decides to sell her car and use the institution's van for trips to the grocery store, shopping mall, church, and medical care providers? Letting go of one's automobile, when she has been an independent driver and car owner sixty or more years, is traumatic. It can be the biggest change in one's life beyond a spouse's death—from freedom to loss of independence.

In my own mother's case, when the time came to dispose of her dependable Oldsmobile, we stood at the automobile's side. She signed the transfer of title form over to the used car sales manager of a major automobile dealership. While he attended to office details, I led in a prayer of thanksgiving for the car's reliable service and of release to a new, unknown owner. With one hand on her shoulder and the other on her car, I asked for divine care as she moved into a new travel routine with the retirement center van. Later, I sent her a note of encouragement and attached a record she had made nine years earlier when the car was purchased. Seeing it through, however, was a bittersweet transition.

When a pastor resigned suddenly from his congregation, after several years of pastoral service, he determined not to return to his pulpit. There was no reception, no celebration of his work, only abandonment and the forsakenness of a cut-off. In calling, I asked him to consider our telephone conversation an act of affirmation. We spoke of his future story and of a therapeutic regimen to help him unpack anger and grief, to strengthen his self-worth, rebond with his marriage partner, and renew his personal connection with God. Mid the crumbling, tearing, and shredding of his career, he claimed that act of friendship to help shore up his future.

Recall with me the experience of the fifty-four-year-old grand-mother, Jan (chapter 1), who was moving from the *householder* stage of life toward the reflectiveness of the *forest dweller*. A lovely farewell party in her honor was given by her secretarial colleagues. Her work "family" gathered for refreshments, speeches, hugs, and farewells. A gift of remembrance was offered. It became a symbol of sustenance and new beginnings.

Gifts representing new life, richness of relationships, cherished social ties, or fresh starts may be given at such times of moving on. Candles may be lighted. Foods representing new life—sprouts, nuts, and seeds—may be served. A plant may be given to beautify one's new workplace or living arrangement. By such means, strength is given for change, and meaning is provided toward transformation on life's journey.

RITUALS OF RECOGNITION

So many instances of achievement, accomplishment, and realized dreams have been noted here. Schoolteachers have recognized pupils' achievements with certificates of merit, citations for good work, grades for citizenship, and trophies of recognition for excellence. Prizes have been awarded for the best science fair entry, the best picture in art, or the most creative essay composed in a language arts class.

Coaches have long known that building teamwork and school spirit is linked to school colors, banners, bonfires, trophies, plaques, caps and clothing with school name, athletic team jackets with sports letters, and gifts of symbolic mascots. Ritual recognitions inspire one's best and challenge coming generations to excellence.

The Nobel prizes in Stockholm, Sweden—presented to literary, medical, and scientific achievers—and the coveted Peace Prize inspire humankind's positive initiatives and renewed efforts for the common good. With hard effort and discipline, Olympic champions "go for the gold" (or silver, or bronze) medals in each event. Olympic presentations do more than glorify a sport or celebrate an athlete's achievement. They note a nation's contribution to excellence and justice for all. They help the world community "hold the center" mid turbulent epochs of war, disruptive acts of violence, and injustice. Olympic recognitions pull history toward celebration and survival. They applaud the world's youth as the future story of humankind.

Not all of us are privileged to participate in great causes such as the Peace Corps, USAmerica's space program at NASA, or a Jonas Salk's discovery of polio vaccine. You may never have a street or building named for you, a musical program at Lincoln Center performed in your honor, a product endorsed with your name, or a historic date noted for you. Still, a school can recognize a scholarly faculty member's research and writing. A hospital can acknowledge a surgeon's "miracle." A publisher can mark a major literary production. A congregation can pause in the flow of life, pinpoint staff ministers' achievements, praise good work, then move forward in worship and mission for God.

Parents can pull bewildered adolescents toward center with newly documented boundaries, assure fresh respect by increasing responsibility, reward achievement with the gift of a special trip, or confer forgiveness with a warm hug. A medical team may sustain a child facing misfortune with a distinguished visitor's visit, a gift, or a musical program of recognition.

How might family rites of recognition work? The parents' gift may be permission to travel with a group, work and earn spending money, or purchase a treasured vehicle (item of clothing, video game, or CD). A daughter can have a "date" for lunch with dad; a son can make a trip with his father as recognition for a next step in life. A grandparent might provide a trust account or travel tickets, or bestow a favorite heirloom on a young adult graduating from college. A family council ritual might be begun or renewed.

Marriage ceremonies have served as rituals of recognition in world cultures for thousands of years. Patterns vary from simple ceremonies—for instance, Indians tying a couple in a hammock in the San Blas Islands—to highly ritualized ceremonies for royal couples in great cathedrals. From plain tribal rites to elaborate religious rituals, men and women have pledged themselves in covenant to each other for life. Such a marriage rite is fleeting. But "becoming married" requires a lifetime of growth and adaptation in all seasons.

From rites of circumcision to religious confirmation, from the Jewish bar mitzvah to Christian baptism, from carenotes to common meals, rituals of recognition abound. They extend a hand to steady a person or family walking through some valley of loss, confusion, wondering, or new beginnings. Such rituals extend blessings in periods of transition and embrace persons made lonely by life's mysterious movements. They point the way toward the future in life's story.

RITUALS OF WELCOME

Ralph Waldo Emerson once said the only real gift is offering a portion of one's self. Ritual acts of welcome are a wonderful way to anchor new beginnings—from births of newborns to receiving immigrants from other lands. Welcomes extend tenderness, affection, playfulness, and the offer of assistance to newcomers and strangers.

Here is a model letter to a newborn child by a caring minister. It exemplifies the ritual of welcome. Such tokens become part of the enduring legacy of a baby's book of remembrance.

Master Chase Carson Kemper
c/o Dr. and Mrs. Carey Kemper
5604 Ridge Road North
Anywhere, USA

Dear Chase:

Welcome to Planet Earth, April 29, 1996! You made a long trip before arriving safely in the home and hearts of Darla and Carey Kemper, your wonderful parents. It was February 24, 1990, when we greeted your big brother, Paul. He is six years old now and will have to get use to having you around as his little brother and new friend.

A little child is the freshest gift from the hands of God that I know. So, your being here just before Mother's Day is a wonderful present.

Your parents are special people. You will get to know them real well. They are buzzing around right now trying to make sure that you are okay and that mother is well. You will like all the nice smells, soft touches, and warm words they have for you. Getting used to other people will take longer. In fact, some people are hard to feel close to or even like, so you'll have to be patient as you make your way into their lives.

Everything isn't perfect in this place. So please take it easy on us grownups. God's great Spirit will keep you within His care. You can count on Him. I pray that you shall have

His light through all the darkness and His love through all the years of your living. Jane and I enjoyed visiting with you last evening. Tell your mommy and daddy how much we appreciate them. The enclosed gift is for something special for you.

Devotedly Your Friend,

Bonds may be formed with newcomers in one's neighborhood by providing a list of neighbors' names, addresses, and phone numbers. A temporary resident may be provided a telephone directory and guide to shopping, medical, dental, legal, and educational resources. An invitation to a casual block party or formal reception, particularly at seasons such as Christmas when one is new in a city, extends welcome. One's office workers may arrange a reception and video the rites of welcome for a new boss or colleague. Some cities have a newcomers' service to introduce merchants, products, and city services to new residents. Gift certificates can welcome a new homeowner to a community or aid in the formal installation of a new minister in a congregation.

RITUALS OF INITIATION

The process of being formally introduced into an office or made a member of an organization is customarily recognized with rituals of inauguration, induction, installation, and investiture. From baptism by a congregation to initiation into a fraternity, from regal investiture of kings and queens to USAmerica's inauguration of a newly elected chief executive or political officeholder, cultures celebrate introductions of new leaders, members, and achievers. The purpose is not interrogation of one's fitness. Inquiry's hurdles have been crossed. Rather, the formalities celebrate both one's achievement and accountability in a new position. A person is thereby presented to a larger community and made known.

Rituals such as these are suggestive, not exhaustive. They do not force change but focus it. Ritualized events help us to name and remember experiences, gather strength for the journey, and move forward. They educate the young, inspirit mid-adults, and fulfill the dreams of elders. Rituals, meaningfully observed, can provide moral force and fiber for the next step of personal or social history. They are the cords that bind our future stories into the universal story of humankind.

SUGGESTED READING

Allen, Jimmy. *Burden of a Secret: A Story of Truth and Mercy in the Face of AIDS*. Nashville: Moorings, 1995.

Allenbaugh, Eric. *Wake-Up Calls*. New York: Simon and Schuster, 1992.

Anderson, Herbert and Kenneth R. Mitchell. *Leaving Home*. Louisville KY: Westminster/John Knox Press, 1993.

Anderson, Herbert and Susan B. W. Johnson. *Regarding Children: A New Respect for Childhood and Families*. Louisville KY: Westminster\John Knox Press, 1994.

Angelou, Maya. *Wouldn't Take Nothing for My Journey Now*. New York: Random House, 1993.

Arnott, Kathleen. *African Myths and Legends*. New York: Oxford University Press, 1989.

Barber, Benjamin R. *Jihad vs. McWorld: How Globalism and Tribalism Are Reshaping the World*. New York: Ballentine Books, 1996.

Bennett, William J., ed. *The Moral Compass: Stories for a Life's Journey*. New York: Simon & Schuster, 1995.

Bianchi, Eugene C. *Aging as a Spiritual Journey*. New York: Crossroad, 1982.

Blanchard, Ken, et al. *Empowerment Takes More Than a Minute*. San Francisco: Berrett-Koehler Publishers, 1996.

Bly, Robert. *Iron John*. Reading MA: Addison-Wesley, 1990.

_____. *The Sibling Society*. Reading MA: Addison-Wesley, 1996.

Bramlett, Perry. *C. S. Lewis: Life at the Center*. Macon GA: Peake Road, 1996.

Bridges, William. *Transitions: Making Sense of Life's Changes*. Reading MA: Addison-Wesley, 1980.

_____. *Managing Transitions: Making the Most of Change*. Reading MA: Addison-Wesley, 1991.

Buford, Bob. *Halftime: Changing Your Game Plan from Success to Significance*. Grand Rapids MI: Zondervan, 1994.

Capps, Donald. *Agents of Hope: A Pastoral Psychology*. Minneapolis: Fortress Press, 1995.

Carlson, Richard and Bruce Goldman. *Fast Forward: Where Technology, Demographics, and History Will Take America and the World in the Next 30 Years*. San Francisco: Harper Business, 1994.

Chandler, Russell. *Racing Toward 2001: The Forces Shaping America's Religious Future*. San Francisco: HarperCollins, 1992.

Cole, Thomas. *The Journey of Life: A Cultural History of Aging in America*. New York: Oxford University Press, 1991.

Couture, Pamela D. and Rodney J. Hunter, eds. *Pastoral Care and Social Conflict*. Nashville TN: Abingdon Press, 1995.

Covey, Stephen R. *First Things First: to Live, to Love, to Learn, to Leave a Legacy*. New York: Simon & Schuster, 1994.

Coyle, Neva and Zane Anderson. *Living by Chance and by Choices: How to Respond to Circumstances and Make Decisions with Courage and Clear Thinking*. Minneapolis: Bethany House, 1994.

Dittes, James E. *The Male Predicament: On Being a Man Today*. San Francisco: Harper & Row, 1985.

Dorff, Francis. *The Art of Passingover*. Mahwah NJ: Paulist Press, 1988.

Fowler, James W. *Faithful Change: The Personal and Public Challenges of Postmodern Life*. Nashville: Abingdon Press, 1996.

Friedman, Edwin. *Generation to Generation*. New York: Guilford Press, 1985.

Gates, William H. III. *The Road Ahead*. New York: Viking Division, Penguin Books USA Inc., 1995.

Gilligan, Carol. *In a Different Voice*. Cambridge MA: Harvard University Press, 1981.

Glaz, Maxine, and Jeanne Stevenson Moessner, eds. *Women in Travail and Transition: A New Pastoral Care*. Minneapolis: Fortress Press, 1991.

Goleman, Daniel. *Emotional Intelligence*. New York: Bantam Books, 1995.

Gould, Roger. *Transformations: Growth and Change in the Adult Years*. New York: Simon and Schuster, 1978.

Jamieson, Kathleen Hall. *Beyond the Double Bind: Women and Leadership*. New York: Oxford University Press, 1995.

Karttunen, Frances. *Between Worlds*. New Brunswick NJ: Rutgers University Press, 1994.

Kaufman, Sharon R. *The Ageless Self: Sources of Meaning in Late Life*. Madison WI: University of Wisconsin Press, 1986.

Kegan, Robert. *The Evolving Self*. Cambridge MA: Harvard University Press, 1982.

Killinger, John. *Christ and the Seasons of Marriage*. Nashville TN: Broadman Press, 1987.

Kotre, John and Elizabeth Hall. *Seasons of Life: Our Dramatic Journey from Birth to Death*. Boston: Little, Brown, and Co., 1990.

Lapsley, James N. *Renewal in Late Life Through Pastoral Counseling*. Mahwah NJ: Paulist Press, 1992.

Leeuwen, Mary Steward Van. *Gender and Grace: Love, Work, and Parenting in a Changing World*. Downers Grove IL: InterVarsity Press, 1990.

Lester, Andrew. *Hope in Pastoral Care and Counseling*. Louisville KY: Westminster/John Knox Press, 1995.

Levinson, Daniel J. *The Seasons of a Man's Life*. New York: Alfred A. Knopf, 1978.

Miller, Calvin. *A Covenant for All Seasons: The Marriage Journey*. Wheaton IL: Harold Shaw Publishers, 1995.

Moffatt, Betty Clare. *Soulwork: Clearing the Mind, Opening the Heart, Replenishing the Spirit*. Berkley CA: Wildcat Canyon Press, 1994.

Morley, Patrick M. *The Rest of Your Life: Your Personal Plan for Finding Authentic Meaning and Significance*. Nashville TN: Thomas Nelson, 1992.

Naylor, Thomas H., William H. Willimon, and Magadalena R. Naylor. *The Search for Meaning*. Nashville TN: Abingdon Press, 1994.

Neugarten, Bernice L. "Interpretive Social Science and Research on Aging," in Alice S. Rossi, ed. *Gender and the Life Course*. New York: Aldine Publishing Co., 1985.

Oates, Wayne E. Luck: *A Secular Faith*. Louisville KY: Westminster/John Knox Press, 1995.

Papp, Peggy. *The Process of Change*. New York: Guilford Press, 1983.

Parks, Sharon. *The Critical Years: The Young Adult Search for a Faith to Live By*. San Francisco: Harper & Row, 1986.

Peck, M. Scott. *In Search of Stones: A Pilgrimage of Faith, Reason, and Discovery*. New York: Hyperion, 1995.

Peterson, Eugene H. *Answering God*. San Francisco: HarperCollins, 1991.

Ratliff, J. Bill. *When You Are Facing Change*. Louisville KY: Westminster/John Knox Press, 1989.

Roberts, Howard W. *Pastoral Care Through Worship*. Macon GA: Smyth & Helwys, 1995.

Roof, Wade Clark. *A Generation of Seekers*. San Francisco: Harper San Francisco, 1993.

Sheehy, Gail. *New Passages: Mapping Your Life Across Time*. New York: Random House, 1995.

Sinetar, Marsha. *Do What You Love: The Money Will Follow*. Mahwah NJ: Paulist Press, 1986.

_____. *Ordinary People as Monks and Mystics*. Mahwah NJ: Paulist Press, 1986.

Stone, Naomi B., et al., eds. *The Asian Journal of Thomas Merton*. New York: New Directions, 1973.

Straub, Richard O. *Seasons of Life Study Guide*. New York: Worth Publishers, Inc., 1990.

Strasser, Stephen and John Sena. *Transitions: Successful Strageties from Mid-Career to Retirement*. Hawthorne NJ: Career Press, 1990.

Sweet, Leonard. *Faithquakes*. Nashville TN: Abingdon Press, 1994.

Thornton, Edward E. *The Christian Adventure*. Nashville TN: Broadman Press, 1991.

Trent, John. *Lifemapping*. Colorado Springs CO: Focus on the Family Publishing, 1994.

Vanauken, Sheldon. *A Severe Mercy*. San Francisco: Harper & Row, 1977.

Wall, Kathleen and Gary Ferguson. *Lights of Passage: Rituals and Rites of Passage for the Problems and Pleasures of Modern Life*. San Francisco: Harper San Francisco, 1994.

Walrath, Douglas Alan. *Frameworks: Patterns of Living and Believing Today*. New York: Pilgrim Press, 1987.

Wiesel, Elie. *All Rivers Run to the Sea*. New York: Alfred A. Knopf, Inc., 1995.

Wuthnow, Robert. *Sharing the Journey: Support Groups and America's New Quest for Community*. New York: Lexington Books, 1994.